PURPOSE DRIVEN

PURPOSE DRIVEN

APPLYING FAITH IN THIS COMPLEX WORLD

Kelly James Martin

Purpose Driven

Copyright © 2021 by Kelly James Martin. All rights reserved.

No part of this publication may be reproduced, stored in a retrieval system or transmitted in any way by any means, electronic, mechanical, photocopy, recording or otherwise without the prior permission of the author except as provided by USA copyright law.

The opinions expressed by the author are not necessarily those of URLink Print and Media.

1603 Capitol Ave., Suite 310 Cheyenne, Wyoming USA 82001
1-888-980-6523 | admin@urlinkpublishing.com

URLink Print and Media is committed to excellence in the publishing industry.

Book design copyright © 2021 by URLink Print and Media. All rights reserved.

Published in the United States of America

Library of Congress Control Number: 2021917339
ISBN 978-1-64753-928-3 (Paperback)
ISBN 978-1-64753-930-6 (Hardback)
ISBN 978-1-64753-929-0 (Digital)

04.10.21

CONTENTS

Dedication 7
Occupational Hazards 9
Developing the Concept.. 11
Adventure Awaits 21
Seeking New Direction 34
Opportunity of a Lifetime... 38
Life continues... 49
A Priceless Gift 51
Trust 55
The Conflict 63
Your Journey 74
You cannot overcome it alone... 76
About the Author 79

DEDICATION

I would like to dedicate this book to Sarah, my granddaughter who is an avid reader. Also, to Judy, my dedicated wife and encourager; the one who inspires me to keep moving forward through all of life's circumstances.

OCCUPATIONAL HAZARDS

◆

I watched helplessly as the upside-down aircraft burned. The horror of the whole scene left me stunned and would be etched in my brain forever. Standing on the wing of a small piston-powered airplane I tried to determine what model aircraft it was. It was obvious this aircraft had been involved in training; I had seen it land and takeoff numerous times as we conducted a preflight inspection on our own airplane. I was not sure what model aircraft it was, only that it had turbine engines. Having fueled many of them in a previous job, I was familiar with the different types; nevertheless, it was not important right now.

What was important right now was this burning hunk of twisted metal that probably had occupants inside who were in an unknown state of being. Randy, my student on this particular day, was getting into the pilot's seat, the only entry door being on the right side of this Piper aircraft. His friend and his 5-year-old son were in the back seat, already strapped in for the approximately thirty-minute flight back to our home airport in western Oklahoma.

Me, I was absolutely frozen as I stood on the wing and stared, trying to evaluate what led up to this dire situation. I knew the propeller was barely turning on the left engine, the only engine I could see from my vantage point, so I surmised the aircraft was on a training flight. What had gotten my attention was the fact that the aircraft had drifted toward the ramp where we were parked and it appeared it was lined up to land on the taxiway. At only 50 feet of altitude, there was a sudden increase in sound as power was apparently increased to the right engine. To my horror, the nose pitched up and this slow-moving airplane turned over, hitting the ground with the nose and one wingtip simultaneously, the crumpling metal becoming compacted ...then, fire! No big explosion, just fire! The jet fuel that had previously been burning inside the engines was now about to consume this destroyed aircraft.

In those days before cell phones, one could only hope that someone inside the terminal building saw what was happening and would call the fire department. Our 5-year-old, watching all this, was no longer a happy passenger. Each one of us was horrified by the whole scene as we witnessed the firetrucks quickly respond. Now it was beginning to make sense, those phrases that my parents used to tell me, like "enjoy childhood while you can" and "don't grow up too fast".

I had dedicated many hours to earn the title of Certified Flight Instructor. Did I have what it takes to be successful in this occupation of flying airplanes?

DEVELOPING THE CONCEPT
◆

The world is such a wonderful creation. Watching the science channel, one can get a pretty good idea of just how immense our universe is, as well as how small a part of it we, as earthlings, are. As a child, just having the opportunity to climb in the car (a Rambler station wagon is the one I remember the best) was a chance to see new places outside of my little world.

"Why did God make so many kinds of trees? "Why did he create the different animals, some that were loveable pets and others that were to be avoided?" "Why can't I see God?" These were all questions I would ask and, I have to admit, are still things I wonder about at times. The world was so amazing that I do not remember ever questioning the existence of God.

Through the miracle of birth we were placed in this world, you and me, and given a free will. We can believe in the Big Bang Theory or we can have faith that God created each one of us for a purpose. I choose the latter, although I oftentimes question just what that purpose is.

Another question that arises is whether we can recognize that purpose so as to strive to fulfill it. What drives you? Are you here to make a lot of money and become famous? If so, what do you want to be famous for? Are you here to raise the next generation? Are you here to serve your country? So many questions …did The Good Lord want us to be questioning? That is all a part of the free will that God gifted to us. That is why he left us an "instruction book" in the form of a Bible.

Now I was raised in a Christian home, but I was not the ideal kid. I can remember being criticized or perhaps called names by another boy at recess and ending up in a physical battle. This did not happen just once, but several times. I always felt bad afterwards (not just physically, but in my conscience). Usually the kid and I were friends again within a couple of days. Does God want us to fight for what we believe in?

As I realized, attending high school, that my growth rate seemed to be much slower than most of my friends, it was natural for me to choose a sport that I could compete in on an even-steven basis. Receiving encouragement from a friend, I chose wrestling. There were a lot of injuries related to football; wrestling matched us according to weight, so I had a reasonable chance of being competitive.

One evening during practice, as I was playing the role of "the enemy", a noise like a "snap" came from my back. Coach immediately urged the other wrestler off, saying "let him up!" "I'm okay, Coach", I responded. Next morning, when I tried to get out of bed, I could barely move without feeling an intense pain.

The doctor, after examining me, admitted me to the hospital. In the hospital, I asked God, "Is this part of what I must endure to fulfill my purpose?" Although it took a couple weeks to recover from the injury, my faith that God would heal me came to fruition. My next match, in a triangular meet, pitted me against not one, but two of the toughest wrestlers I had yet come up against. When these two guys from Nebraska's ranch country weren't wrestling humans they were wrestling bulls! Just looking at them, you could tell they had no fear and they were very confident in their abilities. I only lasted a few minutes with each one of them before getting "pinned", later learning that they earned first and second place at the state match.

In my search for God's plan for me, I was willing to try just about anything – of course, homework took priority. I was not the brightest kid in class, but I strived to do well. Spelling is probably where I excelled. Of course, I had additional motivation; his name was "Dad". My earthly father would regularly talk to me about "when you are in college…", then suggest areas of possible study. My ambitions being rather short-sighted, all I wanted to do was survive until high school graduation.

Like many young people, I liked to have spending money, so I looked for any opportunity to earn that money. Working for a plumber, I gained a general knowledge of what that profession entails. Some days I would come home covered in dirt from crawling underneath houses.

In a later endeavor, I was the dishwasher at a local hotel restaurant. That's a job that seems to go unappreciated; it seemed that way to me, at least. I was enrolled in the junior college at that time. The job was incentive for me to strive for good grades in my classes.

My dad, having a strong work ethic, did all he could to instill that in me. He set high standards for me and for my siblings. One summer, he arranged for my brother and I to work hauling bales of hay for Mr. Franklin, a local farmer. I am sure Mr. Franklin had his doubts when he agreed to pay these two wet-behind-the-ears kids somewhere close to six cents per bale to do the job. He made sure we knew how to drive the 1949 International Harvester truck with a standard transmission. Then he handed us some gloves and the steel hooks we would need to "grab" the bales with, reminding us that he did not want to deal with any injuries due to carelessness with those potential weapons.

He recognized on day two of our employment that he failed to show us a basic farm technique as he eyed our fallen-over haystack. We had much respect for Mr. Franklin and so we got right to work restacking, this time "tying the bales" the way this aged and experienced farmer instructed us. It was hot summer and we wore muscle shirts or no shirts, sweating profusely below the hats we wore to shade our faces. It was hard work and we were physically worn out by the time we ran out of daylight and headed home to take a shower.

A hazard of this job was the possibility of encountering a rattlesnake, as they are not uncommon in the Nebraska Panhandle. My faith was reinforced in that The Lord protected my brother and I from such an evil creature. We saw snakeskins, but I am sure I would remember if we had encountered a live, slithering, unhappy reptile.

My father was a source of wisdom and principle, never wavering in what he believed in. I felt very fortunate, or shall we say blessed, to have him as a role model. He had served in the Army during World War II, although he did not talk about it very much. Dad was an inspiration and I had no doubt about his wishes for me to have a bright future. Matter of fact, many young men are missing that in their lives and my wish to any young person reading this who may not have a father in their life would be that they seek out a person such as that, whether it be a grandparent, a church member; perhaps someone in the Big Brothers or Big Sisters organization. Seek the wisdom of those who have gone down the path of life. {*for wisdom is better than jewels, and all that you may desire cannot compare with her. Prov 8:11, RSV*}

With an attempt not to get too critical here, I would like to send a message to any young person willing to listen with an open mind. I would encourage them to put down their electronic devices and pay attention to all the potential sources of inspiration that surround them in their daily lives.

My mother, bless her heart, is a small woman with gray hair; in her nineties now, she uses a walker to get around. Just seeing her on the street, one would have no idea that she is a survivor of World War II. I have no doubt that, in some way she, along with her sister and mother, was a recipient of the Berlin Airlift. What a story of faith she has to share with any willing listener!

Even today she remembers "slithering under the furniture along with my sister, to hide from the Russian Soldiers who would take anything they wanted from the German civilians". There was no love between the Germans and the Russians during World War II, and

Berlin was not a nice place to be. She remembers times of standing in line for hours just to get a loaf of bread.

Imagine the faith it took to, three years later, climb aboard a ship for a destination called "America" that she had only heard of or read about. Nobody there to send her off, my mother climbed aboard, having faith that this vessel would transport her, over the course of several days, to a new country and a new life. It would bring her closer to the possibility of joining her sister who, weary of war and uncertainty, had already made the trip to the United States. My grandmother would eventually make that same journey, complying with the rules to become a U.S. Citizen. This was her reality; the evil she experienced in a war-torn country would haunt her memory for years.

On the ship, she can remember being assigned a cabin with four other females, also refugees, and since she was used to the top bunk in her small apartment, she volunteered to take the third berth. One of those fellow travelers was dealing with depression, having left everything behind. My mother tells of "tricking her" by saying everybody has to report on deck. My mother knew it may be a once-in-a-lifetime opportunity, and she did not want the young lady to miss the sight as they passed by the Statue of Liberty. She knew it was a very special opportunity and she didn't want anyone to miss it.

The journey didn't end there; all immigrants had to go through processing. Whatever that involved, I can only guess, but she had to figure out how to board a train bound for California. That is where her sponsor, her Aunt, resided and would be waiting for her arrival. Funny, how she always told it to us, "I woke up in the middle of the night as they were announcing arrival into Sidney. In my half-awake state, I nearly panicked, since the only Sydney I knew about was in Australia. We were in Nebraska, the conductor assured me."

It wasn't long after settling in at her aunt's house that she gained employment as a stenographer. She was not what one would call completely fluent in English at the time, but she could converse in the language. Unlike my grandmother, who we called "Mutti" (short for Mutter), my mother had learned the English language in school.

The Aleutian Islands became very important after the bombing of Pearl Harbor, so the Army sent many troops there to defend our shores. My father was one of those. I am sure he was aware of the seriousness of that situation. He had interrupted college to become a part of the U.S. Army, although he did not talk about his service very much. It was the first time since the war of 1812 that our troops had to fight an enemy within our shores. Does one have to have an extra high level of faith to go into battle in the carrying-out of orders that so many servicemen and servicewomen have done?

As I and my siblings got older, Dad would sometimes say, jokingly, "I married the enemy". My mother didn't see the humor in that; she considered the Russians to be the enemy. Many times, as I heard her tell the story, she would talk about how "we only wanted to survive each day ...and we were hoping and praying that the Americans would reach us before the Russians did." Their faith was tested each day of that survival.

How about those who do not have faith in God? How do they even get through each day? If one is an atheist, what meaning is there to one's existence? Why tolerate the trials and tribulations of life in this world? Have most self-proclaimed atheists not experienced any significant trials in this world? Maybe they don't see the need to live with morals or they are rebelling against the principles that were forced on them at an earlier time in their life. Perhaps they have lost their purpose.

Just watching the daily news, one can see that there are many who are victims of misfortune. Each day, there are people killed in automobile accidents, shootings, storms, etc. How many of those whose lives were taken had faith that God would watch over them? I wish I had an answer to that one. If you lose a loved one unexpectedly, it requires much faith to believe that The Lord is going to bring you through it. I know some who lost parents at an early age. I have a heart for those and I believe it would take a tremendous amount of faith to recover from such a trauma.

Feeling very blessed to have both my parents in those early years, I was determined to make them proud of me. I mentioned earlier a job that I held while attending junior college. My parents didn't have the money to send me to college and I was not smart enough to earn a scholarship. I obtained the necessary grants and educational loans, following my father's advice. I kept an open mind, but was not sure of what direction to go nor what occupation to pursue; all I knew was that it would not involve public speaking.

One should look at those who have gone before, as we are instructed in Proverbs 10:17. He who heeds instruction is on the path to life, but he who rejects reproof goes astray.

Earlier, I mentioned the need to have a positive influence in a person's life. In addition to my parents, my aunt and uncle served that role. It wasn't just because they were successful people, in my eyes, but because they were sincere people who emanated respect for each other, as well as a dedication to The Lord. They always seemed to have my best interests in mind, and they were a source of much wisdom.

If I may stray from my story a bit, I would like to emphasize to any young person to seek that person or those persons who you respect and/or admire. Maybe they are someone you are in touch with only occasionally. Be bold and let them know why you hold respect for them. Maybe even ask them for advice at times. As one of those in the "older generation", I can say with confidence that I would feel honored with such a compliment and would act in a way to deserve the respect put upon me. Also, I would consider your sincerity, being likewise sincere and share any wisdom I may have to contribute to your successful future.

Going back to the positive influences in my life, I must give proper recognition to my cousin, Tom. Don't ask me why, but I was one of those rare males who kept a diary in my younger years. Being an introvert, perhaps it was the need to be understood, should The Lord take me out of this world.

Regardless, there is an entry I found, after all these years, that has a big exclamation mark at the end of it. My cousin Tom, who had his pilot's license, took me and my sister flying! This generous gesture by my cousin who I always looked up to (no pun intended), was to have a major impact on my life. More on that later.

Another entry in that same diary reveals the frustration I went through in obtaining my first car. I was going to spend my life's savings (all $450 of it) on a 1963 Galaxie that I saw advertised in the want ads. My parents, of course, educated me on what it costs to operate a vehicle and they convinced me to delay the purchase. Finally, seeing my determination and probably becoming tired of my complaining, Dad worked out a deal in which my younger brother and I would finish the payments on his car. Then, my dad would purchase what ended up being a 1972 Chevy Nova that had a smaller engine, for him to drive the 20 miles each way to work. Promising to be responsible, my brother and I got the 1967 Pontiac Executive with the 400 cubic inch engine that sucked large quantities of gas. Hey, I could haul a lot of my friends in it, sometimes accepting small contributions that went towards the gas bill.

I was involved in the local Methodist Youth Group, a bunch of kids, including myself, needing supervision and help in setting worthwhile goals. In Proverbs 15:22 it says, "without counsel purposes are disappointed, but in the multitude of counsellors they are established." I had those counsellors in my aunts and uncles, several cousins, and particularly, my father and mother. Reverend Bacus was another I must give credit to.

Young people, keep in mind: *you are an influence on somebody, whether you like it or not.* People of influence can be positive or they can be negative. Make the choice to be the former, the positive influence on those who see you and perhaps look up to you.

So my father, who regularly told me to "get that 4-year college degree" probably was not thrilled to find out that I wanted to pursue an aviation career, although I took classes in business, also. Nobody from my economic background becomes a Professional Pilot unless they join the military. Flight training is very expensive. On career day in high school, I had talked to an Air Force recruiter who laid it straight; you have almost zero chance of flying with your nearsightedness. Therefore, I had to change my focus, find a different career to pursue. Even so, I worked enough hours to pay for flying lessons and earned my Private Pilot Certificate.

In the formative years, I was the kid who loved climbing. We climbed the foothills for recreation, once startling a Golden Eagle as I approached the cliff. I will never forget how beautiful that bird was as it took off and gracefully flew away. When I was in my own yard, I would climb different trees in the row of mature cottonwoods. I loved climbing as high as I could, then just sitting there on a branch and taking in the view. Drinking alcohol or getting high, I thought, were potential roads to nowhere.

Having a Pilot's License was a way to get high in the literal sense. I didn't have to own an airplane; I could rent one by the hour at the local airport. It was a whole new world and one that was enhanced even more when I finally got the job I had applied for – at the airport, fueling airplanes.

Keep in mind that I was in pursuit of whatever it was God intended for me to do with the rest of my life. I had no musical talent; I did okay in sports but had no chance of obtaining a scholarship in any sport; math was challenging and rewarding, but I did not feel I had the math skills to become an engineer. "Lord, I could use some help …could you send me a sign, maybe steer me in the right direction?" I believe it was Robert Frost who wrote, "The Road not Taken". He basically describes the turmoil one goes through in making decisions, particularly those that will impact the rest of your life.

In this situation, one needs to pray and to have faith that God will reveal His plan for one's future. Proverbs 3:5 instructs us to Trust in the Lord with all your heart…

In first Peter 4:10 we are instructed about spiritual gifts. Do you have the gift of speaking? That's not me; I was a shy kid who trembled just at the thought of public speaking! Now, speaking into a microphone with no visible audience …that I could do!

I would be lying if I told you I was a natural at flying an aircraft. I did have a high level of determination and I had internalized my father's words of wisdom, "whatever worthwhile endeavor you pursue, do not quit!" If there is any phrase I would like to put in bold type, that is the one. So, through paying attention to my instructor and perseverance, I learned how to fly a single-engine Piper Cherokee well enough to earn my license. Limiting my social life so I could work the hours necessary to cover the costs of lessons, I obtained my goal. They even gave me three hours of credit at the college for this.

As a matter of fact, I would have to transfer somewhere in order to get a 4-year degree. Having been living at home (Mom and Dad's home), my debt was low enough that I was able to pay back all that I had borrowed by the end of the following summer. How could I pursue this goal when I did not have the resources to pay for two more years? Work at minimum wage until I can save enough? Borrow the money to accomplish my goal and work as a Flight Instructor to pay it back? At the time, there was no college in my state that offered a degree in Aviation.

You want to attend college at a place where you have to pay out-of-state tuition? On top of that, you think you are going to handle the added expense of aircraft rental? My father must have thought I was nuts. He could see my determination and my willingness to take business classes in addition, so he did not discourage me. I guess the fact that I was motivated to continue my education convinced him to relent, to let me pursue my new goals.

ADVENTURE AWAITS

◆

Leaving for college, I began the 14-hour drive to what would be the start of a new adventure. There was plenty of time to think, as I experienced feelings of both anticipation as well as those of self-doubt. When you start a new pursuit, do you experience those feelings? My belief is that, if you don't, you may not be committed to succeeding or else you may be in denial. Most of us need some kind of support, especially when we "leave the nest" for the first time. We can't do it on our own. 1 Corinthians 13 says to "be watchful, stand firm in your faith, be courageous, be strong."

My first week in college, I learned of the death of my good friend from high school, George. He was the one who welcomed me when I first moved to a new town, offering to go riding on the bicycles. This was a friend who always had a smile, who liked having fun, who all my classmates held in high regard. This kind of thing wasn't supposed to happen. Why would God take the life of such a wonderful and young individual? I was devastated. Did I have the faith to continue on, there, in this new environment where I knew almost nobody?

I was invited to a party where young men were being recruited for joining a fraternity. Needing to break out of my depression, I decided to attend two of these (shopping, so to speak), although all I knew about fraternities was what I had seen on television, most of it quite negative.

When I found out a particular fraternity emphasized high standards on academics and that it supported St. Jude's Childrens Hospital, I was in. Being in Oklahoma, two states away from home, it was too expensive to drive home very often. This was a group of guys – from several parts of the U.S. - that I could hang around with and build bonds with. Okay, I admit, they also had events with the "Little Sisters", a group of young ladies who supported the fraternity. Missing them, I was used to having my two sisters around.

One evening, I was building those bonds, watching a movie with two of my cohorts, fellow pledges Carl and Greg. As the first movie finished, I thought about the test I needed to study for. I parted company and left the student union building, heading below the streetlights for the approximately 2-block walk towards my dormitory. When you are, as I was, a "pledge", it is like a fraternity brother wannabe. You have limited rights and you must earn your way into fraternity membership. One thing you want to avoid is being caught by a member on campus without the 2-feet-long wooden paddle that identifies you as being a pledge of a particular fraternity.

And so it was, when a pledge of a rival fraternity, apparently leaving a party, saw and greeted me. Approaching closer, he realized his mistake and quickly changed his demeanor. Next thing I know, this scruffy-looking, bearded monster is scowling and is right in my face, telling me how much he dislikes my fraternity. Now, my friend Carl is a Marine who puts up with guff from nobody and I'm hoping he or Greg happens to be looking out the window of the building I just left. At the same time, I am evaluating how large this guy is who now has his hand on my throat and is looking down at me menacingly. He is not a guy I want to scrap with, easily outweighing me by 40 pounds or so. My attempt to talk my way out of the situation is fruitless and I dropped my oak paddle as he lifted me off the ground, tearing my jacket.

He tore my jacket!! That is where I lost my cool and switched tactics. I was on a tight budget, trying to get through college, and this thug thinks he can tear my jacket! Ever watch The Incredible Hulk? Well I didn't split out of my shirt, but I pushed on his chest with both hands, at the same time calling him a name that I don't want to repeat here.

Having now dropped me, he was off balance and I, having dropped my glasses, recognized I was in for the fight of my life. As I saw him coming at me, fists flying, I did the only thing I knew to do; I went for the takedown. He wasn't expecting that move and I managed to knock him down. Now my sister (or perhaps both of them) had always accused me of being hard-headed. I don't deny it. As I thought of every move I had learned in wrestling, I could feel the fists repeatedly hitting the back of my head. The two of us rolled off the sidewalk and up against a parked car next to the curb. My back was up against it and he was facing away from me when I saw my opportunity. My right arm was free. This drunk and crazed beast was about to learn about hypoxia. I reached around his neck, pulling tight and cutting off his oxygen supply. When I felt the grip he had on my hair loosen, and realized he was choking, I let go. After all, I had no intention of killing the guy; I was just defending myself.

Standing in the background through all of this was the guy's friend who seemed to want no part of this. Now shaking from the adrenalin flow, I located my glasses, keeping an eye on this guy, in case he wanted more. His friend urged him away.

"Why, God, does life have to be this hard?" I'm an easy-going guy with a positive attitude and a love for life. I don't go around picking fights. Still a bit dazed, I next headed to my girlfriend's dorm, knocking on her door. Surprised to see me, she had a stunned look on her face, seeing my torn jacket and dirt all over me. I told her about what had just happened.

I'm man enough to admit that I was scared, at least up to the point where my jacket ripped. Once again, God had given me the skills I needed to get through a tough situation. Reflecting silently, alone in my dorm room that night, I wondered if I had what it takes, ie: did I have the fortitude and determination it took to earn that degree? Was this a sign that I wasn't following God's will for me?

I am convinced that God has a sense of humor, and he gave us the same to help us out. In the next few days, as word of this incident spread, I not only felt like I was my girlfriend's hero (she did not like most of the members of that particular fraternity), but I gained many points with my peers. They even jokingly coined the nickname "Killer" for me, as my normal demeanor was quite calm. Many years later some of my colleagues still call me that.

Eventually came graduation day, the day I looked forward to because I could say, "Dad, I got that degree!" It was so important for me to be able to report that news! It's a sense of accomplishment that is so rewarding, as it is the culmination of much dedication and many late nights of studying.

I left college for that new job that a fellow graduate referred me to. Again, those feelings of anticipation and of self-doubt were experienced. My girlfriend (a different one, now) was still in school. When I came back to see her a few weeks later, it seemed someone had taken my place, so I was on my own. Looking at the large debt I had incurred, I felt I was not in a position to be married and raising a family, anyway.

Now I had to get settled in and concentrate on carrying out my life's dream in my new position as a Certified Flight Instructor. Maybe I could get my 1970 Chevelle to last a few more years, although it already had a bit over 100,000 miles on it. Frugality was something I had learned to be good at, by this time.

So, sharing an apartment with a fellow pilot, I embarked on this new career, driving my worn-out Chevy and praying regularly for The Lord to bring me back from each lesson conducted with pilots of various skill levels. My level of faith was quite high at this time, believing the philosophy that so many pilot's hold. It is best expressed by that sign I remember next to the road as you exit the Bartlesville, Oklahoma Airport. It states, "you are about to embark upon the most dangerous part of your journey – the ride into town."

There is material for a whole book, just on the experiences of being a Flight Instructor, especially after enduring through 35+ years in that position. I just want to share my personal opinion in that flight instructors are perhaps the most under-appreciated and underpaid professionals. Matter of fact, teachers in general need to be revered and shown appreciation for their dedication to the cause.

Back to the subject of faith. I want to share with my readers just one occurrence that really tested my level of faith. During a frustrating time of struggle where I had to accept a job as a warehouse worker so I could pay my bills, I was presented with an opportunity to fly on the weekends to make a few extra bucks. The job entailed flying skydivers in a very old twin-engine airplane. It was a great chance to keep up my proficiency as I continued to look for a more professional job.

My friend, Mark, who I consider to be very intelligent, was considering doing the same ...until he looked in the aircraft. This 1950 some model aircraft looked like it had been pulled out of a scrapyard, stripped of all seats except the pilot's seat, and the door, no longer there, was now a doorway, just behind the right wing. The airplane was typically referred to as the "T-Bone", which I will have to do some research into before I can tell you the reason why. Officially, it was a Beechcraft Twin Bonanza. Looking at this one, it was easy to understand why they wanted to jump out, I thought. "This one is used exclusively for skydiving, but the magnetic compass and the fuel gages work", they told me.

Also, the pilot must wear a parachute. That's like telling me it's equipped with a panic button. Only in a complete and utter panic would I ever exit an airplane that was not on the ground. Mark had made up his mind, but I was desperate enough to build flight time in my logbook that I agreed to be their weekend pilot.

The Jumpmaster, a Viet Nam vet, had made thousands of successful jumps. Therefore, I was open-minded, considering what they suggested in at least making one jump. I went up in the single-engine Cessna to observe a skydiver go out the specially-built door into the vast space below. As he quickly disappeared, I noticed my grip tightening on whatever I was holding onto, and my heart rate increased. "You know, the wings on this airplane are still attached – I have no motivation to go out that door. If the airplane catches on fire, I know where the D-ring is on my chute and I'll read the directions on the way down."

I had spent all day, one particular Saturday, making numerous short trips in both airplanes. Speaking to Bob, the other pilot and the one who had checked me out, I said, "ready to call it a day?" Bob replied in response, "no, they want to go up for one more." Trying to talk him into taking this last flight, Bob informed me that he wanted to make one jump, meaning he would be one of my seven passengers. Two young skydivers who had made a few jumps already wanted to go along on this one for the ride.

I insisted they verify the actual amount of fuel in each wing tank, wanting to add a few more gallons. No fuel truck at this small Oklahoma airport, so we would have to drag the 55-gallon drum with the hand pump over, and that was a lengthy process. The wind was absolutely calm and I noticed the visibility wasn't as good as a haze set in, the sun not much above the horizon.

I gave in and agreed to just one more flight. This was in the years before everybody had cell phones and, since there was no control tower, I had no way of verifying the actual visibility. We would be circling over the airport the whole time, anyway ...what could go wrong?

So we launched, doing my job of communicating our position for any other aircraft to hear, then, following normal procedure, I switched the radio to Air Traffic Control. Broadcasting to them that we would be climbing to 9,500 feet and dropping jumpers in about 5 minutes, I noticed how much hazier it looked than when I had observed it on the ground.

Straight down, out that doorway, they could see enough to tell me what direction to turn, and by how many degrees. The idea was to circle directly over the jump zone. Looking into the sun, I can remember thinking that this is going to be challenging because I couldn't see anything on the ground by this time. "It would be great to be in a helicopter right now".

"Jumpers away!" the jumpmaster announced as they were departing the aircraft. I then repeated that same announcement to the ATC controller who would know of any other aircraft that might be in the area. As the pilot, you can "feel" the aircraft get lighter when you lose approximately 80 per cent of your payload in less than 3 seconds. Since this old, worn-out airplane did not have the automatic direction finder needed to receive the signal coming from the beacon on the airport, my next goal was to find the airport with its single runway. "Look for the rotating beacon (the light)", I told the two guys who were still with me, "it should be turned on by now."

Once the skydivers were out, the procedure was to pull the power to near-idle, lowering the nose at the same time, to begin a wide spiral toward Mother Earth. Realizing that there was nothing on the ground that looked familiar, I leveled off at 2,000 feet above the ground. Empty feelings started setting in and I wondered just how long the fuel supply would keep these two engines running. "See anything?" I asked the guys in the back, to which I think I heard the reply, "No, I can't see _____!" Banking left and right in an attempt to get a better look at the ground, I was finally able to pick out the lights of a group of houses.

Continuing in that direction, more houses appeared, so I was confident I knew what direction I had to go to get to the airport. What a relief! Shortly arriving over the place where a runway should be, I realized that this was the next town over, similar in size, so we needed to go west. The compass was the one piece of equipment I could trust in this flying contraption. I turned to a heading of 270 degrees, or west, expecting to see the headlights on the highway below to lead me to the airport. The sun was quickly disappearing below the horizon.

I have to think back to those guys and gals who are trained as paratroopers in our armed services, for whom I hold so much respect. Imagine parachuting to the ground, some who landed behind enemy lines, then having to pick up your heavy load and fight your way to whatever goal your commanding officer set for you. Not only would you have to have faith that your parachute would open properly, but I believe you would need a tremendous amount of faith in your fellow soldiers and in God to keep you from harm. One bullet, one shard of metal entering your body could alter your life forever ...or end it.

No bullets to dodge, life was good for this pilot, now knowing where I had to steer this thing in order to get us home. ...Then, the right engine lost power!

I think my heartbeat took a short pause, then I quickly went into "situational awareness" mode. That is a term used in aviation (and other occupations, I feel certain), referring to your ability to realize where you are in space and what options you may have at your disposal. More thoughts went through my head in the next 20 seconds than I had thought in the last month! Looking out of the corner of my eye, I remember thinking, "these two have jumped before ...why are they still on board?"

The engine surged, indicating that it was probably running out of fuel. In any case, <u>why</u> it was giving out was not important. The surging made it difficult to control the airplane, so I shut that engine down. As fast as the visibility had dropped, I thought, "Is this where you remove me from this life, Lord?" I don't have much altitude; I don't have the airport in sight, let alone the car lights on the highway below; there is a high probability that the only remaining engine could run out of fuel at any second. I momentarily entertained the thought ...yes, you guessed it... I was wearing a parachute. I have no doubt that, if I left my seat and headed toward the doorway, these two would be out before me. Then, if I did that, would the airplane continue, uncontrolled, taking out some innocent commuters on the highway who are completely unaware of the situation?

The decision-making came with no doubt as to what I had to do. In the murkiness, I spotted a field below, announcing, "brace yourselves, I'm landing in the pasture." They could do what they wanted at this point; I was busy and focused. Pilot training serves the purpose of preparing pilots for moments like this. Usually, I was the one suddenly reducing power and telling my student that his or her engine quit; "what are you going to do next?"

Of course, thoughts of that burning aircraft I had seen months before entered my mind with the knowledge that those pilots survived, thanks to some very capable firemen who were nearby with fire-fighting equipment. Landing in the middle of nowhere, this flight had to have a better outcome. There was no room for error.

I removed any remaining power, then lowered the landing gear and extended the flaps. Seeing a tree row at the other end of the field, it was obvious that we did not want much airspeed as we made contact with the ground. I can remember hearing a "thump" just before feeling the tires of the main landing gear make contact. Pulling way back on the yoke to keep the nosewheel off the ground as long as I possibly could, I felt the airplane bounce along on this rough surface, and we decelerated to 30 miles per hour. Then, the sudden stop, as if we had just hit a brick wall.

Any part of me above my waist lurched forward from the momentum and I hit my lip on the control yoke. Looking out the windscreen, I now saw grass and dirt, as well as the nose gear mechanism that had protruded through the top of the nose. I had not had much time to evaluate the situation. My lip was bruised, but there I sat, still strapped in as the adrenalin flow kicked in. When I should have been thanking The Lord for being alive, I was instead, cursing the guys for wanting to take this one more flight. Matter of fact, I think I may have recited every curse word I knew in two different languages, then switched to condemning myself for not insisting on more fuel. I was shaking so badly by this time, it is doubtful I would have been able to walk for a couple minutes.

Oh, yes, the two passengers – did they jump? I turned around to see them sitting on the floor of the airplane, silently listening to my blurtings of condemnation. "Are you okay?", I asked, to which they replied "Yes, we're fine". To this day I don't know what kept them from flying past me and into the front panel when we made the abrupt stop.

So, the three of us, in the twilight, exited the airplane. Parachutes on our backs, we examined the rise in terrain that caused our nose gear to collapse, then we headed through the pasture in the direction we knew to be towards the town.

My guess is it was approximately a mile to the farmhouse we first spotted. In that walk I had time to think, remembering the phrase, "ye of little faith…". I imagined Jesus standing before me saying, "why did you even doubt that I would bring you through it, alive and well?"

I had to admit, the bruised lip I received was insignificant, considering what could have happened. As we approached the farmhouse, we had to climb over a barbed-wire fence. Seeing a white van entering the driveway, we waved and tried to explain to the suspicious driver who we were and why we were there. Imagine seeing three strangers approaching your house, parachutes on their backs, and you have no idea where they are coming from.

The homeowner accepted our story and was gracious enough to give us a ride into town where we could use a telephone to call the owner of the airplane to tell him the bad news. By the way the farmer made mention of his Doberman and how it was a good thing he drove in at that time and it wasn't the Doberman who first greeted us. It did not seem funny at the time, but I later imagined newspaper headlines reading something like, "pilot survives emergency landing; gets mauled by a Doberman."

The aircraft owner, glad to finally hear from us, said, "where are you? We'll come get you!" When I divulged the information about the damage on the airplane, he told me, "Don't worry about the airplane ...I have it insured. Glad you guys are okay."

My next concern was with the FAA. I had dealt with the FAA a few years back while flying out of the Denver area. Not knowing how to deal with a government official hell-bent on condemning a young pilot, I gave him everything he needed to suspend my license. The letter I wrote to defend my actions included an admission of guilt, even though the other airplane was at no time in danger of a collision. "Honesty is the best policy" was the phrase I had learned and what I tried to live by. When I finally located a lawyer, the damage was already done. The crime was an altitude violation, roughly equivalent to turning a car into the wrong lane and correcting before traffic conflicts.

As it turned out, that same lawyer was able to plead my case on this occasion, as I refused to talk directly to the FAA. My lawyer told me they were not overly concerned as there were no injuries and the aircraft damage was below a certain monetary level.

What should you do, when faced with adversity such as this? Should you quit? I spent many hours reviewing my career goals, considering whether maybe I should go a different direction.

Again, that self-doubt that can tear at you like a ravenous beast that wants to destroy you. Luke 11:9 tells us "Ask, and it will be given to you; seek, and you will find; knock, and it will be opened to you." In my process of seeking, I was not finding that ideal job as a Professional Pilot.

Still driving that 1970 model Chevy, seven years after graduating from college and having an equal number of years left to pay on my educational loans, I was frustrated with my position in life. I felt obligated to fly skydivers the following weekend, in the single-engine airplane; however, I had many thoughts about how much time and money I had committed in my pilot certificates. Do I want to continue this risky weekend job in old, worn-out airplanes? One thing was certain in that I needed to raise my standards on what aircraft I was willing to operate.

Time to talk to the recruiters at the Air National Guard! Even if I couldn't fly with them, I would be around airplanes and would be serving my country. My dad and both uncles had served during World War II. I had much respect and admiration for them. This is the direction I want to go!

The physical exam you must take to qualify to join the Air National Guard is quite thorough. I set aside a whole day to accomplish this. To me, this was just a routine requirement, a hurdle to jump, as I rode my bicycle regularly. I was within 10 pounds of the weight I had been in high school; exercising always made me feel better afterwards, so I stayed in good physical shape.

On the day of the exam, I went through hearing tests, eye tests, heart rhythm tests, etc., seemingly doing well. Approximately two hours later, they have me and several guys running in circles in our underwear, when one examiner motioned for me to leave the group and come to where he was standing. "Let me look at your feet," he told me. Standing on one leg, I cooperate and allow him to examine the bottom of each foot. "Did you know you are flat-footed?" he asked. Giving an honest reply, I said "No - what does that mean?"

"It's a disqualifier", he told me, explaining that everybody must go through boot camp and the powers that be think you wouldn't be able to make it with flat feet. "Sorry, it's beyond our control."

I was stunned. In high school I had competed as a sprinter in Track and Field. I even ran a close fifth place behind the four guys who became our mile relay team. That team not only won first place at the State Track Meet, but they set a new record in the process.

There was a historical movie created, called "The Battle of Britain", documenting that time in history when a young group of pilots took on the ominous force of the Nazi Luftwaffe. It's my favorite movie. Yes, I am at least 50% German, but this battle represents the weakening of an evil tyrant who took advantage of his position of power, spreading fear and uncertainty.

It was a blow to his unchecked ego when these determined pilots, outnumbered 10 to 1, took to the skies in Spitfires and Hurricanes, and, one-by-one, managed to destroy a large percentage of those aircraft that were sent to do harm to their home country, England.

According to historical records, 153 of these British aircraft were lost in and around the English Channel at one point, after taking out 562 German aircraft. Some of the pilots managed to eject in time to parachute into the English Channel to be rescued, allowing them to fight again.

So it was, having been "shot down" as I was leaving the facility where I had been tested and rejected. Flat-footed? ...are you kidding me? I really wanted to do this! Feeling like that pilot who had just taken a hit and was spinning toward the sea, smoke trailing behind, I retreated to my rented apartment.

God, what do you want me to do? By this time, many of my college comrades had secured employment with the Major Airlines. I did have some saving grace in finally finding out that the FAA decided to classify my precautionary landing in that pasture as an "incident" rather than an "accident" since there were no injuries, nor did anybody die.

By the way, the "thump" I had heard as we arrived in that pasture turned out to be a fence post; rotted out, it broke as the airplane's right flap hit it. Two strands of barbed wire came with it, leaving just one strand intact. Had I been lucky that day? I refuse to believe that that is the case. "He delivers and rescues, He works signs and wonders in heaven and on earth, he who has saved Daniel from the power of the lions." Daniel 6:27

That spinning aircraft I referred to earlier can be brought out of that spin if the pilot follows the instructions of The Instructor. He must have faith in those instructions that he must force the nose further in a nose-down direction when everything in himself wants to pull the nose up, towards the horizon. The Wise One, in the best interest of the student's survival, imparted his instruction to do what is necessary to break the stall on the wings. By doing this, having faith in The Instructor, along with proper pressure on the rudder pedal, one can save himself from the death spiral and begin flying under control again.

Ask yourself the question: Are you following instruction or are you just wandering through life? The Bible, in Proverbs 4;13 tells us, "Keep hold of instruction, do not let go; guard her, for she is your life."

SEEKING NEW DIRECTION

◆

Feeling alone and wondering if anyone cared whether I was successful or not, I stayed the course, being responsible with loan payments, faithfully showing up for work at that warehouse. Like the pilot in that damaged aircraft, now separated from his comrades and flying level, just above the English Channel, staying on a constant course gave him hope that perhaps he could limp back to his homeland.

My friend, Mark, also pursuing an aviation career, called me one day about an opportunity. He was taking a job flying a corporate jet and asked if I would be interested in the position he was vacating, as a charter pilot. Of course I was interested, so I arranged to meet the Chief Pilot, the one in charge of hiring. This turned into the opportunity I was looking for, the chance to apply my flying skills in a position that would further my career. Flying charter flights meant traveling to many different locations in a variety of airplanes. The missions usually involved passengers, but sometimes we would haul freight.

One mission assigned to me was particularly important. The freight I carried was a pair of kidneys that had been donated. I assume a match had been made and these kidneys needed to be transported to a hospital in Cleveland. Charter pilots don't receive much warning for an assignment such as this one. Preparation time is minimal. Fog was engulfing the airport in Cleveland, according to the report I received prior to takeoff in Oklahoma City. The hope was for the fog to lift by the time I arrived several hours later.

The Aerostar was the name given to this airplane, built by Piper Aircraft Company. Shaped like a bullet and having two engines, it was capable of respectable speed. Time was critical. The first two updates from Flight Service were disappointing as I needed to have a certain minimum visibility at my destination. Other airports in the area were reporting better conditions, so I did have them as alternates, at least.

With most other cargo, it would have been fine to land elsewhere and wait for the fog to lift. This mission was different. I tried to imagine how elated the recipient of these kidneys probably was when given the news of his/her match and the possibility of discontinuing dialysis procedures. My role was only a small part of the mission, but doing it to the best of my ability carried an especially high priority on this day.

Approaching the Cleveland airport from the southwest, I was given the latest report which said visibility was now at minimums. Slowing the airplane down, I descended into the low cloud layer and maneuvered to fly the instrument approach. Landing gear down, the control tower has already given me permission to land. All I have to do is find the runway through the fog. 300 ft. …200 ft. …100 ft. Relief! The approach end of the runway finally appeared and I was able to land. The kidneys, in their Igloo cooler, were handed to the driver who would deliver them to the appropriate people at the Cleveland Clinic.

My role in all this was over and I arranged for fuel and filed a return flight plan. I wished I could meet the person who had been kind enough to mark "Donor" on his or her drivers license.

Daily missions were mostly unpredictable in this business. Perhaps that unpredictability was what made it such an interesting job. All I wanted was to reach a point where I could bring in enough income so I could maybe start a family. So many of my friends from college were already raising families.

There was just one problem with this in that I didn't even have a girlfriend at that time. I have to admit, I had developed a distrustful attitude toward females.

There was one exception. I will use the name Amber to refer to her. She was a special person who I felt I could trust. She was fun to be around and would greet me with a smile. There was nothing sexual between us; we had a mutual respect for each other and enjoyed each other's company. We went on canoeing trips and other recreational outings.

Once, after I had accepted a job in a new location, I realized how much I missed her. I managed to get tickets to a football game. Contacting her, I was happy to know that she would meet me for another day spent together. I thought Amber was beautiful, a near-perfect one of God's creations. She was enrolled in college at that time, hours north of where I lived. After the football game we had dinner together. I felt every moment spent with her was precious. We talked about classes and goals and hopes and dreams.

Finally the time came where we had to part and I felt much sadness. I was holding back tears as I gave her a hug, blaming it on the wine. Once a friend, you are my friend forever unless something major happens to cause it to end. I moved to a new location; another attempt at furthering my career. I thought about her a lot, finally surmising that she deserved much better than me. I soon lost touch.

So, where do you go to meet people like this? Probably not in a bar, although I really don't believe there is a hard rule. Many turn to dating sites on their computer, so they can "cull out" the undesirable ones, the ones they determine don't match their interests. They can also eliminate the ones that, in their eyes, don't meet the standards in appearance.

When you go home to visit and your own father says, "there is this girl at work who is unattached…", you know it's about time to think about possibly raising a family. At the age of twenty-eight, I was one of those who went to the internet to find my match. It felt awkward, to be honest. I had, in the past, learned about a girl over a period of time before I ever went out on a date. Somehow, evaluating them on a website and talking over the phone just was not the same.

On our first date, I noticed she had the license plate on her car that identified her as being a Christian. She did attend church regularly and showed respect toward her parents. So, this must be the one intended for me.

Amazing thing it is, what a computer can do to find a "match" for you via a dating website. Age was within a year; same number of siblings; non-smoker. Add to that the fact that both are approaching the age of 30 and are aware of that biological clock ticking. Don't I owe it to my aging parents to give them a grandchild?

We dated for close to a year before I brought up the possibility of marriage. She divulged that she was a divorcee and she claimed to have been abused in her previous marriage. Seeing the pictures of her sister on the wall, I surmised that her sister was the cuter one of the two.

Her sister had taken her own life, as a teenager, which I think must be the most severe level of depression a person can reach. I could not understand that. Even though they claim that a person who turns on the car in a closed garage is hoping to be found; it's a cry for help – they don't intend for it to be fatal.

I had much respect and compassion for her parents who had to live with that. Who are you failing to consider in carrying out an act such as that? How about her younger brother, who, I believe, was scarred for life? Did she even consider what that would do to him?

Serious about the vows we took, we were married at age 29 and it wasn't long before we were expecting our first child.

OPPORTUNITY OF A LIFETIME

◆

This was a new way of life and one that brought new responsibilities. When my wife was approximately 6 months along, my boss offered me the chance to make a flight to Germany. His words were "How would you like to go part of the way on this delivery trip? You will need a passport, if you are interested." Interested? Deutschland! Wunderbar! I can purchase a passport for that! It would involve 4 days getting there, then I would return to the U.S. via the scheduled airlines. Talking it over with my wife, she was okay with it, so I purchased a passport and brushed up on my German.

As so often happens in the aviation business, the mission changed. "By the time they get the required avionics installed, we will be struggling to deliver the aircraft on time," my boss told me. "I need you to go the full route to Japan. The company wants it there by March 31st."

Her parents were less than 20 miles away, so I wouldn't be leaving her there by herself. She told me that she was okay with it, knowing that I would return in approximately 15 days. In addition, my pay for that period of time would be significantly better than if I turned down the opportunity.

On March 21st, I was in the copilot's seat of this Dornier 228 turboprop, leaving Oklahoma City for Tokyo. This would be my first trip out of the U.S.A.

On arrival into Bangor, Maine, we had our first challenge. A current limiter failed and we had to wait for them to locate a replacement. Not quite as common nor as readily available as a circuit breaker, this current limiter had to be shipped from some other city. Having the repair made, we headed northeast toward Goose Bay, Canada.

Goose Bay had experienced a snowstorm recently and there was a large amount of it still on the ramp, as well as walls of it on either side of the road to our hotel. We needed an auxiliary power unit to get the engines started the next morning, then we launched for Narsarsuaq. It was very rough-looking terrain below with no visible signs of life for the first part of this leg. Soon after, we could tell that we were over water, the white caps on the waves below becoming visible between the clouds. Communications are difficult, so some of the required position reports are accomplished through other aircraft near our route. Playing with the HF radio, I was able to pick up the signal from an English-speaking European station. Iceburgs below appeared as chips surrounded by a beautiful blue ring as we approached Narsarsuaq on the southern end of Greenland. It was quite interesting to see the beautiful colors of the glacier. Wondering what possesses a pilot to ferry a single-engine four-seater, I realize the one on the ramp was temporarily a two-seater airplane. The back was now a fuel tank to give them the necessary range for flying many hours over water.

Fueling there, we continued on to Reyjkavic, Iceland. I can remember fish being on the menu there; seems that beef wasn't readily available.

Next morning, we left for Prestwick, Scotland, our official entrance into Europe. It was quite windy there with an overcast sky and spotty rainshowers. I can remember having difficulty understanding the Scottish accent. After fueling, it was on to our destination near Munich, Germany, called Oberpfaffenhofen. The weather over Germany was overcast and all I got to see of the country was from the base of the clouds to the runway. We have faith in our instruments to lead us through the weather to a point where we can visually steer the aircraft to the desired runway.

I have to imagine what it was like, shortly after World War II ended, and the Russians controlled the area surrounding Berlin.

American pilots were flying Douglas C-47's, C-54's, and Dakotas into Berlin's Tempelhof Airport with food and supplies, day and night, in all kinds of weather. It was known as The Berlin Airlift and this operation lasted for close to a year. I imagine the faith it took for the people of Berlin; faith that The Lord would rescue them from the wrath of the Russian Regime.

After shutting down the engines, we met Captain Tom and Gerhardt, both a part of the company Dornier and both who were to join us on this journey. Gerhardt was not a qualified pilot, at least not in this aircraft, but his role was to oversee any mechanical problems we might run into. Captain Tom was a very fit and trim German, quite confident, and it was soon obvious that he was very intelligent. Seeing how tired we both looked, he arranged for us to be transported to a nearby hotel for a meal and a few hours of sleep.

After a rude awakening before sunrise, we are transported back to the airport, where Gerhardt is fastening down luggage and supplies, including oxygen tanks. A short discussion and a change in location of some luggage for weight-and-balance and the airplane was ready for flight. Shortly after takeoff we were donning the oxygen masks. This was an unpressurized aircraft and we had to climb to a high altitude to traverse the Alps. Everything from this point on was new territory for me. Captain Tom, on the other hand, was very experienced and knew the best routes to take.

Alps behind us, we descend to an altitude that allows us to hang up the oxygen masks. In the back with Gerhardt on this leg of the trip, I have the opportunity to get to know more about him. (Only occasionally do I find it necessary to pull out my German-English translator.) "Tech-rep" is what Gerhardt uses in referring to his title. We call him our flight engineer. Unmarried, he apparently travels a lot. He is "head strong" as I would expect this dark-haired Bavarian to be. Outspoken, he is very interesting to visit with.

After a nap to attempt a recovery from the short night, we awaken to sunshine and what I am told is the Greek shoreline. Iraklion, on the island of Crete, was our first fuel stop. As we went inside to file flight plans, check weather, etc. we greeted some American military pilots who were exiting. They were about to embark on their mission, whatever destination that included.

Required quantity of fuel on board the airplane, we departed across the Mediterranean, A few cumulus clouds are all the weather we have to contend with. Next time we see a shoreline, it appears as one gigantic beach, continuing inland with little to no change in color. I look for signs of life. There is a lonely truck traveling slowly along a road that disappears in places; apparently sand dunes. Looking for many miles at this barren land, I wonder how any truck driver might have to deal with any breakdown.

The Nile River Valley is easy to pick out, appearing as a two-mile- wide strip of green. We are soon descending towards Luxor. Captain Tom performs a perfect landing and taxis to the designated spot we are to park. I have a feeling of uneasiness as I see our aircraft being approached by eight or nine military personnel, guns hanging on their shoulders. They asked some questions and glanced at our passports, then made a sweep of the aircraft interior. Seemingly satisfied, they headed back inside.

It is not long before we are all sweating in the heat, especially Gerhardt. It was his job to fill the tanks with jet fuel from atop a ladder. My boss headed in one direction to file a flight plan and Captain Tom decided to make me useful. He reached into the pouch he was carrying and pulled out a $100 and a $10. "This," he said, handing me the 100-dollar-bill, "is for the guy up in the control tower. The other one is considered to be a tip, not to be recorded in the book he will have. I will catch up with you in about 10 minutes."

As I approached the control tower, I noticed each of the three guys standing at the base of the tower was carrying a large firearm. I don't speak a word of Egyptian. It was very intimidating. One of them motioned for me to follow him inside. At the base of the stairs, he turned around and held his hand out, palm up.

Apparently I know some sign language; he was happy to take the five-dollar bill I handed him, but then he pointed to his two cohorts and held his hand out again. I was not prepared for this, as my boss had told me expenses would be taken care of. "Okay, just shoot me," I thought as I showed him my empty billfold. He just turned and motioned for me to follow him up the stairs.

The ATC guy, or Tower Controller, could speak pretty good English as is required for him to be qualified for the job. He smiled and welcomed me, easing the tension, then he offered me a cup of tea. I handed him the bills as I had been instructed, signing on the line that would indicate that we paid the required fee; the $100. Captain Tom soon joined us for a short chat, then we returned to the aircraft for departure.

Flying over many square miles of sand, we head in the direction of Saudi Arabia. I was now in the back with Gerhardt and had my camera out. This was a very inexpensive camera, one that I accepted could be confiscated at any stop by customs officials. I noticed that we made a turn to the south, directly over the Red Sea. The pilots up front informed us that Saudi Arabia would not allow us to fly over their country. We made it to our overnight stop, Djibouti, at approximately sunset.

It seemed that loose clothing was the fashion here. Fueling arrangements made, we realize that we will have to compete with a planeload of passengers heading from a Boeing towards the growing line at customs. Finally through the line, I was amazed at how four of us and our bags were able to squeeze into that small taxicab along with the driver's approximately 6-year-old son. When I got to my room, it seemed to be quite small, too, but I did not care. I was very tired by this time and went to sleep shortly after going to bed.

The next morning we met in the lobby for breakfast. While waiting for my comrades, I notice a bird sanctuary just off the lobby that is behind glass and has netting on top. That peacock that I thought was stuffed is now moving, although it remains perched atop a wrought-iron bench. I am entertained by a bird – perhaps a quail – that is running laps around the perimeter of the sanctuary. All of us present now, we are able to enjoy breakfast from a large selection of fresh fruits and baked breads. Our window allows us a glimpse of the bay through the haze. All discussion is on this next leg of the trip. The goal today is to reach Bombay, after making one fuel stop. Another cab ride and we were at the airport again. We were very appreciative of the fact that this aircraft had air conditioning. This was the southernmost point of our journey and we next headed for the country of Oman. Salalah was the fuel stop today, not far from the eastern border of Yemen. No point A to Point B on this leg of the trip; our flight path looked more like an arc, as we stayed offshore as long as possible.

Another great landing by Captain Tom and we were instructed to shut down a long way from the terminal. The Lockheed L-1011 belonging to the King of Jordan was parked on the airfield, so special restrictions were in force. Maximum fuel was required, as we were about to spend several hours over the Arabian Sea.

On board the aircraft, of course, was an inflatable raft that we hoped to never need. The requirement was for a flare gun to be part of the emergency equipment, so that must have been on board, also. Although we traded off positions being in the cockpit, I was once again in the back trying my best not to think about how poor a swimmer I was. I buried my head in the Book of Baby Names I had taken along. The agreement with my wife, before departure, was to narrow my choices down to 3 or 4 top picks; we would compare notes after I got home, to see if we agreed on any.

On this leg, realizing how many miles we were from home, I came to realize the importance of having the faith that The Good Lord was going to bring me safely home from this trip. I was soon to be a father!

We started seeing the lights of what was then Bombay (now Mumbai) as we approached the shore. Increasing numbers of lights appeared. There seemed to be a million of them, as the city appeared to cover a vast area. As we touch down on the brightly-lit runway I have a high level of curiosity towards this city and its people.

Another attempt at getting a good night's rest is crushed as we spend a ridiculously long time waiting for the customs official to arrive. When he finally shows up and progress seems to be made, another official comes along and starts an argument with the first in his native tongue. We just stand helplessly by. Finally they seem to reach an agreement. We are then transported by bus to some office where we filled out paperwork and received the required stamps on our passports. As we were transferred in the back of a jeep to the hotel, I wonder whether I had made a wise choice to go on this mission.

What I soon discovered was that the captain had secured rooms for us in a 5-star hotel. It was like we were arriving in Oz as our driver pulled into the paved, flower-lined entrance. A brightly-lit lobby area, uniformed bellmen and beautiful, smiling hostesses in long dresses made me wonder if we were going to see the Wizard.

I admired the colorful decor as I ascended to my room on the eighth floor. Quickly cleaning up, I then met the others in the lobby for our dinner meeting. Southbound to Sri Lanka was our next planned leg.

An early breakfast the next morning and we are inside a bus being transported back to the airport. Many people on foot or on bicycles are going in numerous directions on the street. The driver beeps the horn frequently to warn pedestrians ahead. Just outside the airport terminal are several lines of taxicabs waiting for arriving passengers, however we are taken to where general aviation and our airplane are. We disembark, go inside to clear customs, then climb onto a different bus to be transported to our parked aircraft. Preflight accomplished, we start the engines and request clearance from the ground controller.

Heading south after departing the runway, the terrain is quite mountainous. I notice much terrace farming on the hillsides. We find ourselves over water again and Captain Tom gives me a brief report on the conflict that has been going on in Northern Sri Lanka. That fighting won't be anywhere near us in Colombo. Approaching that coastal city, I am in awe of the lush greenery. I discover that coconut trees grow in abundance here.

As expected, it is hot on the ramp while we wait for the fuel truck to arrive. We surmise that the fueling crew is busy with a Singapore Airlines Boeing 747 that has just arrived. Also, we notice what appears to be a military C-130 parked approximately a quarter mile north of us. Studying it, Gerhardt recognizes it to be a Russian-built aircraft.

Our aircraft attracts a lot of attention and we allow the curious a peek inside. Of course, all must be outside the airplane as it is being fueled. Gerhardt gives out the last of his Dornier stickers as Tom returns to the aircraft.

I am in the captain's seat as we accomplish the start on the right engine. Oil pressure, etc. are normal, so I begin the same process for the left engine. Left generator does not come on and we are forced to shut that engine down, followed by the right engine. Here is where Gerhardt's expertise is valuable; he determines we need to replace the generator. This is going to put pressure on us to meet our delivery deadline as Captain Tom makes arrangements for a night or two in a nearby hotel. We will have to wait for the arrival of the specially-built generator and an engineer to arrive from Singapore.

We soon find ourselves inside a tiny cab, the driver taking us down the fast lane. The fast lane is the one down the middle of the unmarked road that only exists because of the driver's liberal use of the horn. A right turn takes us down a palmtree-lined drive to the hotel. It is a ten story building located close to the water. The natives are very friendly, the men in loose-fitting light clothing and the women in very colorful full-length dresses.

We check in, each being assigned a room in various parts of the hotel. I feel lucky that I don't have to deal with communications to home base. Colombo is 12 and a half hours different from Oklahoma City. My boss, Curt, doesn't get to spend much time relaxing. Tom knows we will be here a while and he gets to work figuring out a flight path that will shorten our remaining time enroute. There is time for me to go through the shops, finding everything from post cards to a $500 ebony elephant. Having been warned that ivory is an item that will not make it through customs, I carefully pick out and pay for my small souvenirs.

I decide to take a stroll. Judging by the small number of people I see, this must be the off-season for tourists in this area. The rectangular swimming pool on the bay side of the hotel sits unoccupied. I walk along the path that leads toward a covered dock on the shoreline, noticing about a dozen surfboards by the wayside. I try to imagine how active this place might be during tourist season.

When the new generator is installed and tested, the remainder of the journey becomes a marathon, with spurts of flight duty and of napping. Kota Kinabalu, Malaysia; Hong Kong, China. Both these airports I was able to add to my list of destinations. What an education for someone who only had a limited knowledge of the geography of the world!

A day before arriving at our intended destination in Japan, we were informed that a volcano eruption caused the closure of the Kagoshima Airport. That meant that Okinawa would now be the point at which we entered Japan. Landing there, we met the time deadline. Next day we managed to deliver the aircraft to its new home in Tokyo. This was a special aircraft as indicated by the large group of Japanese citizens and photographers that greeted us outside the hangar door.

There was food and drinks and speeches. Smiling faces and celebration were around this tired crew as the aircraft was now in the hands of its new owners. Once more we are brought to a hotel, this one with beautiful gardens around it. That evening was a celebration with lots of food and even a souvenir jacket that was presented to each of us crewmembers.

My assignment being done, the company put me on a flight that would take me eastbound, connecting in Seattle, and then home. First flight for me in a Boeing 747, the Jumbo Jet, as it is referred to. What an enormous aircraft! On that flight, I had time to reflect.

It seems to have become a more common phrase these days, about "living the dream", although sometimes it is used sarcastically. That was me on this flight, "Living that dream that, so often, seemed so out-of-reach." I was so grateful for my dad who had repeatedly told me "DO NOT QUIT!" As for my mother, the more I heard those stories of survival during the war, the more of an inspiration she became to me.

This is the time to consider all the things that had to fall in place in order to arrive at this moment in time; the time to thank God for rewarding me for keeping the faith. Here I was, my first flight out of the U.S, and I am literally circling the globe. In the movies, this would be the point at which they would fly off into the sunset, "happy music" playing in the background.

LIFE CONTINUES...

Do I hear you saying, "I don't have the opportunities that you had"? Perhaps you are thinking, "...but, my situation is different." Of course it is ...everybody's situation is unique! In this high-tech world of ours, it can be overwhelming just deciding what career to pursue or what you desire for the next chapter in your life. As a person who became very independent, I can be sincere in telling you that you can't pursue your purpose all by yourself.

This word "self" is a term referring to one being. "Me, myself, and I". It is part of the word "selfish", described in Webster's Dictionary as follows: *concerned excessively or exclusively with oneself; seeking or concentrating on one's own advantage, pleasure, or well-being without regard for others.*

We are all selfish beings – God made us that way. Watch a group of toddlers sometime and they will prove my statement. At age two or three, it is a major barrier to overcome, for a child to learn to share.

Did you ever know or can you think of someone who is like that in their adult life? Many of those are in prison because of their inability to control their selfishness. Perhaps if a person were placed on their own planet with no other humans then selfishness could go unchecked with no consequences.

Let's imagine a world such as that – nobody to be accountable to. You could eat and drink whatever you want; sleep as long as you want; run around naked if you want. Nobody around to criticize you nor for you to be critical of. Sounds great, doesn't it?

On the other side of the coin, there would be nobody there to treat an injury; nobody to notice any accomplishments; nobody to comfort you when you are sad. If you wanted to confide in a friend, there would be nobody. For some, a day or two on this imaginary planet would be a welcome escape from the chaos of everyday life, a chance to re-assess where you are in life. It might be an opportunity to reset some of your goals or even set new ones; a time to reassess your purpose.

I am confident that there probably is no planet like that, but the islands in the Caribbean do a great job of attracting stressed-out humans in need of some peace and quiet. I have not spent a vacation in the Caribbean. My idea of solitude is being surrounded by mountains, enjoying the scenery that only God could create. The point is that we must each find where it is that we feel that peace and solitude that allows us to reflect.

How about that subject of faith? The Bible tells us, in Galatians 3:26, "for in Christ Jesus you are all sons of God, through faith". Defined by Webster's Dictionary, faith is, among other definitions, "firm belief in something for which there is no proof." The doubters or the non-believers like to emphasize that phrase, "...for which there is no proof". One has to consider, what constitutes "proof"?

I used to question God on why He doesn't bring Jesus to Earth again, in a physical form so that we could see Him and maybe ask him questions that I had so many of. Wouldn't that be "proof"? How would the world receive that? Hebrews 6:18 tells us "by faith we understand that the world was created by the word of God, so that what is seen was made out of things which do not appear."

Humans, in general, have a tendency to want control. Attempts have been made to control even the weather among many other things. Hitler and his Nazi ambitions were perhaps the ultimate example of man's failed attempts at gaining control. My opinion is that he chose to be evil and he refused to accept the blessings that God made available to him.

A PRICELESS GIFT

◆───────

Let's go back to that pilot over The English Channel, retreating with his damaged airplane. He sees that he has the fuel required to make it to a friendly airport. In spite of the fact that the smoke spewing from the engine, now minimal, has not caused a drop in oil pressure, the engine seems to be running okay. The Lord protected him from harm in that brutal air battle that he was forced to retreat from. Although flying at low level, he is below a broken layer of clouds, making him harder to detect by any enemy aircraft. He feels hope now, thinking about friends and family that he will get to be re-united with.

That described me as I was able to be there for the birth of my son. We named him Christopher. This tiny being, this beautiful and wonderful gift from God was like no other gift I had ever received. Holding the little guy in my arms made me feel a special connection to our God, the Creator.

That gift was doubled less than two years later when the next one, who we named Anthony, came along. We were not prepared financially, as Tony's birth was not covered by insurance. I did everything I knew to stay healthy and to accept as many flights as possible to make sure that my wife and my young sons were provided for.

She had to give up her job, so the responsibility was on me. When I pointed out to the boss that I was being paid considerably less than industry standards, it only seemed to irritate him. When that irritation built up to the point where we were not seeing eye to eye, I got fired.

The Bible says, in Proverbs 29:23, "A man's pride will bring him low, but he who is lowly in spirit will obtain honor." This is a difficult one for the pilot who has spent more than five years safely flying numerous models of airplanes in all kinds of weather and at all hours of day and night. I had enough evidence in my possession to file suit against the company, had I been vindictive.

This company, who I had been so dedicated to, had now placed me in a desperate situation. I was feeling frustrated that I had not received even an invite for an interview with the 8 different airlines nor the air freight companies that I had sent resume's to. I had even scrounged up the money to take the Flight Engineer written test which I passed. I was frustrated and angry.

My wife, by this time, was spending most of her time at her parents' house, where they lived in a nearby town. Scouring the want ads, I found an ad for a job I was perfectly qualified for. Just three hours away, I arranged for an interview.

That 1970 Chevelle had been sold by this time, as we needed the money. A good friend and fraternity brother had sold me his old Monte Carlo. It had a strong, dependable engine and four decent tires. I called it my "Green Machine". A 1972 model, it's faded exterior was a dull green with hail dents all over.

Driving to and from my appointment in that vehicle, I had a great interview with the hiring manager and was offered the job. I knew my wife would be relieved and I was anxious to share the news. The firing would be a blessing in disguise, allowing me to apply my skills as an instructor in high-tech simulators. Also, I would be home more.

She was anything but supportive. I explained the benefits package, the immediate raise over what I had been making, the fact that she would only be a 3-hour drive from where her parents lived. I am not fond of moving, but it is sometimes necessary to relocate to where the opportunity is.

Beginning in this new position, I stayed temporarily in the apartment of another instructor whose lease had not yet run out.

An air mattress in a corner, a pan to heat soup in, some essentials for bathing and for washing clothes. It was a very basic setup, but I had a roof over my head. Besides, I got a part-time job at an ice cream shop, so I was gone most of the time, anyway.

Christmas at her parents' house was fun with a one-year-old and a baby. These two were undoubtedly a gift from heaven. It is both interesting and amazing to watch a child of those ages as they learn to interact with adults. Knowing what my wife's parents had endured in losing a child, it was rewarding to see the look of happiness on their faces as they held and watched the babies.

Still not caught up on bills, I returned after Christmas to the two jobs and the house in Kansas, leaving my family there. The agreement was for her to stay in Oklahoma until the worst part of the Winter was past. She had the 2-year-old Nissan to go places and was in a familiar environment. (My parents were a 10-hour drive from the new job location.)

As March brought in warmer temperatures, the situation had not changed; I was still working 2 jobs and coming home to an empty house. Every time I brought up the subject, she found excuses not to move. I asked a fellow instructor if I was being unreasonable in wanting my family close. He told me, "I would have gone down there to get them a month ago."

So, next day off I made the trip. After visiting for about two hours, I told her it's time to go home. The response came as if it were coming from a four-year-old kid. Christopher, who I was holding in my arms, was now getting upset, so I put him down on the floor. Intending to continue the conversation, I went out to my car to put the bag I was holding into it. As I was backing out from the back seat, I felt the car door against my back. I remember turning to see her father standing there. The rest of that day I can only recall in flashes.

Feeling some hands on my arms picking me up from the driveway, I can remember seeing blood and dirt. I could hardly move on my own. I was so confused; I asked the EMT if there was anyone else in the airplane. Still dazed, I had no idea how I got there. I could hear the wail of the ambulance each time I regained consciousness.

Next day, in my hospital room, it was explained to me what had occurred and, "would you like to press charges?" Yes, I filed charges and I looked up a lawyer. Driving back to my two jobs, after being released from the hospital, it was obvious that someone had caused damage to the front end. The vibration was so bad that the left front tire heated up and blew. Hearing metal scraping on the pavement and seeing rubber flying all over in my rearview mirror, I managed to pull hard enough on the steering wheel to bring the car to a stop on the right shoulder.

It took me close to an hour to change that tire. Perhaps it was the pain meds that kept me going that afternoon.

Over the English Channel still, our fighter pilot suddenly took a hit from somewhere, most likely from a fighter of the Luftwaffe, transiting the area. The bullets penetrated the aft section of the canopy, dislodging something metal, which then glanced the back of his skull. He feels intense pain, physically, but his thoughts are on revenge. He increases power and begins a climbing turn, wanting to find the aircraft that took the cheap shot at his already-damaged aircraft.

Then, he gains his senses and throttles back. What if that enemy aircraft was part of a formation? Attacking such a group would be suicide. "The pilot of that aircraft had no idea of my intentions. He no doubt saw me as a threat."

In any case, returning to his original heading was his best course of action, increasing the possibility of his survival. The hit he took did nothing obvious to his engine, although the face of his fuel gage was now broken, making it impossible to determine the remaining fuel. He would have to trust his own judgement, stay the course, and have faith.

I know I looked like hell when I showed up for work the next day with a black eye which didn't heal for several days.

Court cases can be long and boring and I would rather not go into details. I eventually dropped charges, agreeing to whatever the arbitration court came up with. I had no quarrel against her father; I actually liked the man and held respect for him. After all, what would I have done if, like him, I had stepped out of the shop to hear my only daughter screaming bloody murder? I had to forgive.

TRUST

In the last chapter, I mentioned the concept of trust. We put our trust in many things on any given day. We may trust the coffeemaker to make that magic liquid that gets us going in the morning. We trust our vehicle to start and to take us to our workplace. We may punch a timeclock that we trust to properly record our time on the job.

How about those stunt drivers ...I mean the ones who build up speed on their motorcycles to go up a ramp and sail over a group of cars? Is it accurate to say they have a high level of trust in the laws of physics? When I watch these "Masters of the Motorcycle", I have to wonder how many times they missed (maybe how many bones were broken?) in getting to the point where they trusted their own abilities to land properly and not wipe out.

Ask yourself the question, "Do I have trust issues?" In that first paragraph I was referring to inanimate objects. If you drive an old car, maybe instead of the car it's your mechanic who you put your trust in. The best mechanic you can be associated with is the one who either you or a friend has gone to for a long time because you learned to trust his abilities.

Trust is not automatic. Trust can only be established over a period of time, perhaps years. When someone breaks that trust, it takes a long time to build it back up again. Do you consider yourself to be trustworthy? It is imperative, absolutely necessary that you develop that self-trust in order for you to trust others.

Perhaps there is someone in your life who has let you down. If that person is unaware of your distrust, you should confront that person. Do not be condemning because that only leads to defense and arguments. Let that person know about the hurt you experienced or are experiencing because of whatever action caused your distrust. Sometimes pride gets in the way and we, as humans, do not want to show our vulnerability.

If you allow that vulnerability to show and the other person has no compassion or shows no understanding, then perhaps he or she does not deserve your friendship. There are many people in this world of ours and many out there who are deserving of your friendship.

Trying to befriend some foster kids who were temporary neighbors, I recognized how difficult it was to gain their trust. They were passed from home to home, lacking the consistency that so many of us take for granted; that care received from dedicated parents. I have much respect for those who have taken in an orphan or a foster child and given them that needed trust.

Must we, as God's children, have trust in order to have faith? The two seem to go hand in hand. *"to rely on the truthfulness or accuracy of"*. As a noun, *"Assured reliance on the character, ability, or strength or truth of something or someone."* That's the way it is described in Webster's dictionary. If I trust you to pick me up to go somewhere, don't I have to have faith in you that you will show up at the agreed upon time and place?

Think about all the events that had to happen in order for you to be where you are today. Of course, your mother went through the process of birth. That alone should make you grateful. That same process occurred two more times when your mother and your father came into existence. How did they meet and what did they see in each other? Do you have grandparents who would be able to share some stories about the situations that occurred that led up to your birth?

You are, no matter what your situation, a unique individual. If you tell yourself the lie about, "My situation is different, so I couldn't accomplish the things _____ did," then you are creating an escape route that limits your ability to excel. Okay, so I accept the fact that I will never be a professional football player. That was never a goal of mine, even though I loved to play football when I was a young kid. Most people in this or any other country will never be a pro football player. Your goals have to be realistic. Perhaps you are around others who put you down or are discouraging. You don't need that kind of negativity, and I would encourage you to get away from that situation.

The Bible tells us in Proverbs 2:11–13,

> **Discretion will preserve you; understanding will keep you, to deliver you from the way of evil, from the man [person] who speaks perverse things, from those who leave the paths of uprightness to walk in the way of darkness.**

There are too many of those who, for whatever reason, do not want to see you become successful. Believe me, I have seen it many times. The best way to counteract it is to not give up, to resolve and find a way to reach your goal, knowing that temporary setbacks are going to come your way no matter what your endeavor is.

I love hearing the stories of "unsung heroes"—ordinary people who overcome extraordinary circumstances. I recently heard the story of Juan, a Williamsburg teenager who was riding as a passenger in a car that crashed. Juan was ejected through the sunroof, receiving devastating injuries. At the hospital, the doctors gave him a 5 percent chance of survival as he lay in a coma for three days. Even if he survived, they claimed that he would not walk nor talk again. I believe it was his mother who refused to give up, apparently a woman of great faith. She prayed fervently along with many of her friends. Not only did Juan came out of the coma, but he was walking after therapy and could talk again. Miraculous, in the eyes of most.

Then there is David. I only got to know David because I happened to pick the same college as he did. You didn't have to know David very long before it became obvious that he was a man of faith who took nothing for granted, and he had a love for life. We kept in touch occasionally in the post-college years, and during one phone call, I was saddened to hear that he was given a sentence of about a year to live due to cancer he was battling. I recently had thoughts of David, so I tried the number I still had to check on him. Not only did I hear David's voice, but there was obvious excitement in his voice as he shared the trials and overcomings he had experienced since our last communication.

I can only imagine what he and his wife and children went through as they dealt with his battle with a cancerous tumor that had formed in his lung, as well as some in his liver. It got so serious at one point that his family was called in, the doctors believing he was down to only days in this lifetime. David only learned of what seemed to be his fate when his daughter tearfully informed him at his bedside in the hospital. I know David well enough to believe that he was willing to accept whatever the Lord planned for him. I am also a believer that God can and sometimes does perform miracles. David not only made it through the night, but he started showing improvement, eventually putting aside the walker that he had been using to get around. The doctors were amazed as they learned though the tumor was still there, it no longer was cancerous. David continues to be an inspiration and a positive influence to young college students.

Going back to my own situation (...which I share only because I know it so well...) there was an attempt to make family life normal again. Her parents were welcomed into our home. My wife and I located and eventually joined a church, as we agreed that we both wanted our boys to have Christian influences. Visits were made to the zoo, to childrens museums, etc.

We watched the olympic competition one year and the boys learned about medals. When we checked out an extracurricular wrestling club, our youngest one decided he wanted to earn a medal. It was so interesting to observe him as he learned all the techniques necessary to overcome an opponent. He listened and learned and worked at it until he got that first place medal. We hung it on his wall, next to the bunkbed. I was so proud of him!

Our oldest one, Chris, liked to sing, using that toy microphone that he received on his birthday one year for a gift. When he was around seven years old, he sang "Happy Birthday Jesus" in front of the whole church. ...solo, even! I had to wipe away the tears of pride, even though I knew any talent he had was not from his dad.

On one of our vacation trips the boys were in the swimming pool with their "floaties"; you know, the little blow-up devices that you wrap around a child's arms to keep them afloat. In any case, I decided to surprise them with a "cannonball", entering the water near them without any warning. They were very surprised, then so thrilled by that, they begged me to do it again and again, laughing almost uncontrollably each time the splash came their way. To see the boys delighted faces is one of my best memories. It was such a fun time!

Soon after that vacation ended, through a good friend of mine, I learned of a new opportunity. It would involve flying airplanes again and would provide a significantly better paycheck. Knowing that I would be a fool to pass up this opportunity, I applied for the position.

With flight experience in foreign countries on my resume', I was offered the job. This position involved learning to fly jets as well as 3-week-long assignments in foreign countries in single-engine turboprop airplanes.

One particular assignment stands out in my mind. Delivered to a Colorado airport, I was to bring back a small business jet to our home airport in Wichita, Kansas. A bit nervous at first (I was used to having a copilot next to me), I reminded myself that I had been trained to do this. Departing the runway, I retracted the landing gear and made the turn to the east. Climbing to my cruise altitude of 39,000 feet, I had to think back to those days in the cottonwood trees of my childhood, then to my dad's stern face, imparting the wisdom, "Do Not Quit". Looking down on an occasional airliner going by, I somehow felt triumphant. I reflected on what determination and faith my mom had exhibited in her quest to reach America. I wished for the ability to share with my parents the gratitude I felt for all their dedication.

Over the English Channel our fighter pilot is seeing better conditions now and feels confident to climb to a higher altitude. Doing so will offer him a better chance to find and identify that airport he needs to reach. He has thoughts of all those family members who supported him, as well as the tears that flowed down his mother's face as she watched him go off to war. He should be spotting the shoreline of the U.K. any time now. Maybe he is a bit hypoxic; he feels excitement and anticipation. The war is not over; he realizes that. All the same, he is feeling victorious.

The landing in the business jet at Wichita went well and that mission got accomplished. Careerwise, I had nothing to complain about. On the other hand, trust had never been re-established in the marriage. There was just no chemistry. It had become apparent that it was a marriage of tolerance. We tolerated each other for the sake of the boys growing up with two parents. I was starting to notice what should have been little red flags, but I did not recognize the source. Perhaps I tried to ignore it for the most part.

One day I confronted her, asking her why she always let our oldest son sit next to me when we drove to church. Why did she insist on sitting in the back seat? I don't remember getting a logical answer, but I finally figured out it was all for show.

There are some individuals who are always critical and quick to point out flaws in others, although they have little to back their opinions. I started noticing her criticizing even those she claimed as friends. Being married to such an individual can be torture.

I don't recall very many dreams, but there was one that stands out because it seemed so real. It was only a short scene, but I remember this one well. In it, I am standing in a doorway with no door attached. It is nighttime. In the distance is a large, shaggy creature that is lurking; pacing in anticipation of grabbing its prey. I am feeling a terrible feeling of vulnerability.

When I woke up, I could not go back to sleep. The chills went down my spine as I thought about what I had just experienced. If I had owned a gun, I would have readied it as I sat there, trying to analyze what the dream meant. I tried unsuccessfully to delete it from my memory.

Also in my memory was and is the phrase, "even though I walk through the valley of the shadow of death, I will fear no evil, for thou art with me..."

By this time I had been the recipient of a layoff notice. Pay had been good at that job, so we had savings, both in accounts for the boys' future education and in an emergency fund. I spent six weeks obtaining a Commercial Driver's license, then committed another six weeks living in an 18-wheeler, learning why I was not cut out to be a truck driver. I did gain a new respect for those drivers and what they deal with on a daily basis.

Through connections and perseverance, I was able to accept an occasional contract flight and eventually to return to where I had been as a Flight Instructor in simulators.

The boys, by now, were in their teens. Neither one was involved in any type of sport. I still had the '68 Volkswagen Beetle that I had bought after the layoff, having to sell the nicer car that I was making payments on. I took the boys out to some empty parking lots where I taught them how to drive a standard transmission. It was the only "us guys" time I had with them. Their grandfather had pieced together an old truck and given it to them. They would need to gain the skills necessary to drive that beautiful old truck. Drivers Education gives young drivers some basics, but Kansas law required them to get one year of supervised driving experience.

KELLY JAMES MARTIN

THE CONFLICT

◆

It was going to be just a normal day. I was drinking my morning coffee and preparing for work. The boys were getting their backpacks ready for the walk to school. The high school is on the way to work, "why don't you guys ride with me – I can drop you off" I told them.

In the driveway, the youngest one was already in the back seat when the older one (the 17-year-old) came out the door. This vehicle, by the way, was not the old VW that he struggled to control. It was the '99 Pontiac Gran Prix with the automatic transmission, red. It was the one I had bought with the plan to let him eventually inherit once he proved to be a responsible driver.

"Chris, I'm going to let you drive us to school", I said, expecting him to jump at the opportunity. What I saw next completely floored me. "I don't want to!" he exclaimed, as if he were a six-year-old. I had a hand on his backpack to help him remove it so he could sit in the driver's seat. He wriggled out of it, threw it on the ground, then stomped off towards the school. Confused and caught completely off guard by this behavior, I followed him down the street, then let the youngest one out, saying, "Tony, go walk with your brother. He's obviously dealing with some issues and I have to get to work."

Remembering how I would have been thrilled with a chance to drive when I was that age, I wondered what brought on that behavior.

Returning from work that afternoon with plans to have a family meeting after all were home, I parked the car in the driveway, noting the time. Everyone should be home from school by now, except the wife who drove a bus route. Only Tony was there, saying he did not know where his brother was.

Shortly, it became apparent that the older brother had taken a bus over to the bus barn where his mom was. He came in the front door and immediately began removing his shoes. I told him, "Chris, put your shoes back on – we're going to practice driving." By this time his mommy was standing in the door and he was looking at her for cues, as if he didn't know how to respond. "Look at me, Chris, I said put your shoes on!"

His mom has now started to argue with me instead of backing me and the tension in the room was becoming elevated. It was not helpful at all.

Now, I had been an instructor for years and I knew it would be useless to drive with him while he was in this state of mind. This kid was not motivated to learn. All I was doing at this point was trying to get his attention, to get him away from distractions so we could have a one-on-one discussion. I was standing in front of him, making him look me straight in the eyes as I told him, "we'll be gone less than an hour, now put your shoes on."

I felt like I was talking to a zombie, at the same time listening to his mother who was now making threats towards me. The conversation had elevated to shouting, so now the young one gets in the middle of it.

This is where I should have gone to the oldest one's bedroom and started collecting his stash of video games. I didn't. I let pride get in the way and I grabbed Tony, angry that he was challenging me. I forced his arm behind his back, telling him that I didn't need his interference.

Of course, the police show up, one officer getting her story and one interviewing me. What was surprising to me was the question, "Do you want to press charges against your son?"

"No! ...I don't want to press charges against my son! I recognized when things were getting out of hand; that's why you found me in another room. I had separated myself from the situation so everybody could calm down. My plan was to have a civil discussion, but she decided to involve you guys". "I understand", he stated, "but it's my job to ask". He told me that this is considered to be a domestic violence case and we have to bring somebody in. "I suppose that's me", I said, and I cooperated completely with him as he placed handcuffs on me and escorted me to the squad car.

As we traveled the 12 or so miles into town, I heard chatter on the radio. "They are looking for a suspect after a stabbing ...do you see the helicopter?" he said, as he pointed towards the south. He was respectful and friendly.

When we arrived, he asked, "Is this your first time?" I answered him truthfully, "Yes". He explained that I would go through processing where they would take my belt and anything in my pockets. He was very accomodating. I could see where this might be headed, so I asked if I could take a breathalizer test, just for the record. He stated, "There is no reason for suspicion, it's not necessary. You will be placed in a holding cell temporarily, then they will come get you and most likely let you out on your own recognizance". "Okay, thank you", I said, although I wasn't sure exactly what that meant.

The officer's prediction was right, so there I was, approximately 14 miles from home with a bunch of papers in hand, no vehicle, and less than twenty dollars in my pocket. I hired a cab to get me as far as I could afford, then asked the driver to stop and let me out. In the darkness, I walked the remaining 10 city blocks to my home. Unlocking the door, I walked in past my wife who was talking on the phone, told her that we're going to have a family discussion, and I headed for the shower. I felt filthy. Through his bedroom door, I told Tony, "I was never this disrespectful to my father!"

After showering, I was getting dressed when there came a loud knock on the door. "Who is it?" I asked. "It's Officer Smith. What are you doing here?" Puzzled by the question, I said, "I live here. Why are you back?" "You better put your gun down if you have one!" he demanded. I said, "Officer Smith, I don't even own a gun", and I opened the door. He asked me if they gave me some papers and I handed them to him, explaining that it was dark in the cab and I had not read them yet.

This policeman, who was so friendly and professional two hours earlier, barged into the shower room, shoved me up against the sink and placed handcuffs tightly on my wrists. He then forced me up the stairs and out the front door, practically dragging me toward the squad car. I have no idea what was told to him, but he had a completely different personality now and he would not explain anything to me.

Bringing me to the station, he transferred me to another officer's car. My wrists were in so much pain that I had tears running out of my eyes. I leaned sideways to take some pressure off. "Sit up!" came the command from the front. I was completely silent, thinking, "Jesus suffered so much more than this". Next thing I can remember is being placed in a cell with 8 others and I sat on the hard floor in a corner, still in shock. "You okay?" I heard from one of them, to which I nodded.

Some were boasting about how long it took for the police to catch them. I got the impression that they were regulars, perhaps in trouble all the time. The most serious one of the group, a young African-American, stated, "I was just trying to discipline my boy – the only injury he received was from trying to escape out the window. He's going to end up in a gang." I wondered how many fathers, trying to instill discipline, ended up in that place.

Just then, the sound of metal on metal was heard. The door opened and one more young male was added to the group. From across the small cell came, "Dude! ...what the @%*! happened to you? That looks like blood all over your shirt!" "It is", came the reply, and this new tenant boasted about how many times he stabbed somebody; and, how long he was able to evade the police.

I was in utter shock, thinking, "now I get to be in the same room with a murderer." I feel like I am living a nightmare. They switched us to a slightly larger cell and I found a spot along the wall, on the hard floor all night long. My thoughts, at this point were, "Is this where being faithful gets me? Lord, you know how I have been dedicated to my family; you know how I have been kind and always faithful to my wife; you know I have been responsible with my money. I tried to be encouraging to my boys. Why am I here?

I did not sleep at all. I was thinking about how I had been sincere in saying my vows twenty years earlier. Still in shock, I wondered if

I should have stayed home from work that day and found out what it was that caused the teenager's tantrum. In the back of my mind, I always wondered how the abuse she told me about that she had been exposed to from a relative during her childhood affected my wife. I wondered if I had done enough to make her feel safe over the past years.

We had recently made plans to join some friends in a weekend outing, to see a movie. It was a fun movie, not a serious one. I was both confused and disappointed, joining the group after I got off work, that she and the boys had not shown up. I wondered if, when I filed for divorce 18 years earlier, would I and would the boys have been better off if I had gone through with it? I wondered why she had no contact with her older brother, a man of integrity, who lived on the East Coast.

They did not care that I had a client scheduled at my job the next day. I had to learn about obtaining a bond before I could go anywhere. When morning came, I managed to do that, then I hired a cab to get me to my workplace. Looking like hell, I went to my supervisor's office. He looked at me as if a monster had entered the room. I let him know that I was up all night and could make up the time with my client after I get some sleep at a nearby hotel.

This whole situation caused me to need a lawyer for the battery charge, and a separate one for the divorce. I could see all those years of savings going out the window. Also, all those years of dedication to the job and to the family were going unrecognized ...and I was now homeless. Not convicted, only accused. ...and now... homeless. Thoughts that God had forgotten me entered my mind.

That fighter pilot who was holding so much hope hears the engine sputter and then go silent. Although, at that time, research was in progress towards ejection seats for pilots, those were not yet perfected. He would have to crawl out after opening the canopy if he was going to have any hope of survival. The trick would be missing the tail, as it could knock him unconscious or break bones or worse.

Now catching sight of the British shoreline, still too far away, he turns the aircraft to parallel it. With no power left, he does not have to bring the nose up very far to slow the aircraft to a near-stall.

Having never done this before, it was just instinct for survival and he was now putting complete trust in God to deliver him. Then he climbs out.

Through those first few days, my friend Doug was invaluable. He and his family so kindly gave me a place to stay. I experienced that dream again – the one with the evil creature in it. Not at Doug's house, but usually as I was daydreaming, waiting my turn at the courthouse. It would jolt me to consciousness every time, sending chills up my spine.

Speaking to my lawyer one day, he informed me of a program that was in place for first-time offenders. "You're a perfect candidate for this", he told me. I could volunteer for this several-week course on "Anger Management". Realizing I was stuck in the system with few other options, I, of course, volunteered to sign up. On approximately the third session, the young man who was the program specialist said, "I deal with derelicts and substance abusers regularly. You don't belong in this program."

He signed me off for completion, highly recommending me to see a professional for the depression. She was a psychologist, an older lady who was a therapist specializing in family counseling, and he held her in high regard.

Depression, for me, had been a temporary feeling that I was always able to overcome in a short period of time. I guess that's why I never really understood it. This was a new thing, a darkness that had its grip on me. It gave me feelings of not only sadness, but of self-incrimination as well. This whole situation was very overwhelming and I scared myself one evening, while driving to my empty apartment, with thoughts of suicide.

I tried to think happy thoughts which did help for short periods. Doug and his family were encouraging. He pointed out a particular verse in the Bible, Romans 5;3, which says, *"we also glory in tribulations, knowing that tribulation produces perseverance and perseverance, character, and character, hope."* I tried to etch that phrase into my brain.

Knowing that I needed as much help as possible, I set up a time to meet with the pastor of my church. He was encouraging and he asked me if I would like to help him with some projects around the church in my spare time. It was just what I needed. While painting, he and I had some good heart-to-heart talks.

Every time I showed up for a court appearance, I would end up in that pit of despair. I showed up without a lawyer once. Dressed appropriately, I was on time and was very respectful ...the judge wouldn't even give me two minutes before he put me off, ordering another session for two weeks later. What a waste of time! The system had me in its trap! How was I ever going to climb out of this pit?

It is depressing to even write about, but depression is a real circumstance; a serious situation. It can cling to you like a sticky substance, sucking the life out of you. Trying to appear happy on the outside, you are crying on the inside, wishing to hide or to disappear from the world.

I made myself attend church, knowing that I needed to keep that connection. I was told that the boys' mother asked the ushers to remove me from the church. They refused, but I stayed as far away from her as I could.

Not wanting to cause friction, I called my pastor to let him know I would only attend the Wednesday service so as not to create any conflict. I wanted my boys to keep that connection. Two weeks later, my pastor told me, "She isn't bringing the boys on Sunday, nor is she attending anymore." I continued attending anytime my work schedule allowed.

Knowing how difficult it is in today's society, is it such a terrible thing to want your kid to be able to handle a vehicle responsibly? I had thoughts about how, in the past year, she one day informed me "the boys don't like food cooked on the grill". Also, on those Saturdays that I was home, she would try to take them shopping with her rather than letting me spend time with them. I had noticed it, but I didn't know what to do about it.

Apparently, I was the "mean dad" for insisting that Chris remain at the table until supper was over when he tried to sneak off to his room with his plate of food; for making the boys stay home one Saturday to learn how to change the oil on that old truck.

Why had I not seen all this happening and recognized there was a serious problem? I believe psychologists have a term for it, "parental alienation". I blamed myself. These were not the kinds of problems my dad ever had to deal with. I had always shown respect for him, knowing how he always had his family's best interests in mind.

Dad was always dedicated to his employer, as I tried to be. Anytime I did something to disappoint him, I would feel devastated. It meant a lot to make him proud of me. I lost him at age 83, starting a whole new chapter in my life.

Pastor Boone, being completely honest with me, said, "You know this could take a long time to heal, perhaps years". I was horrified at the thought. Raising these guys for the last 18 years was the majority of my purpose in life. What would I do? How would I cope?

Back to our fighter pilot, who has now separated himself from his aircraft. He tumbles uncontrollably at first, but then realizes he somehow managed to miss getting hit by the tail. He now sprawls, stretching his arms and legs out, as he was taught in order to stop tumbling, then deploys the parachute. There is a sudden deceleration as it deploys and he can see his aircraft hitting the water close enough to shore that they might be able to recover it.

Hoping for boats to be nearby, he sees none. The Mayday transmission he tried to make over the radio just before he bailed out went unanswered. Had anybody heard it? It seemed he floated under the parachute for less than a minute before splashing down in the cold water of the Channel.

Still dazed, he knows he must cut himself loose from the chords of the chute and he wishes for a bright light that he could use to signal someone. It is now dusk and he does not know how long he can last out here …and he prays another prayer.

Thinking again about that phrase from Romans, "tribulation produces perseverance…", I had to wonder why I needed to persevere and in what direction. There, again was that frustration and depression setting in. It felt like I was treading water and slowly sinking the whole time. "Lord, why do I have to go through this torture? One day I even tried using alcohol to drown the pain, but, after passing out, I woke up feeling worse. Alcohol is a depressant and it's the one thing a person needs to avoid in this situation.

Thinking of all my friends and my mother and my siblings, I knew suicide was not going to be an option; they were in this battle with me. I would go down fighting, if I went down. There was Pastor Boone and Debbie, Doug and Tami, Peggy, Bill and Christi, Mike and Karen, Darin and Tina, Pastor Merle, Nadine, Chuck, and others I could call or otherwise contact.

Proverbs 27;17 says, "As iron sharpens iron, so a man[woman] sharpens the countenance of his[her] friend." Another way of saying that is that you need friends in order to maintain mental composure; ...to help you climb out of the Pit and re-establish your purpose.

One thing I have always believed in is continual learning. I had heard of a local Toastmasters club and had recently joined. These were aquaintances at that point, but I took the therapist's advice to continue attending the meetings. They were becoming friends and I was learning each time I attended.

Many days I was living on faith alone. There were more sessions in court, more bills than ever to keep up with, and I wasn't eating very well. While reading one day, I found a quote that seemed to fit so well. I printed it and framed it and it became my only wall-hanging. A quote from William Lyon Phelps, it stated, "You can be deprived of your money, your job, and your home by someone else, but remember that nobody can ever take away your honor.

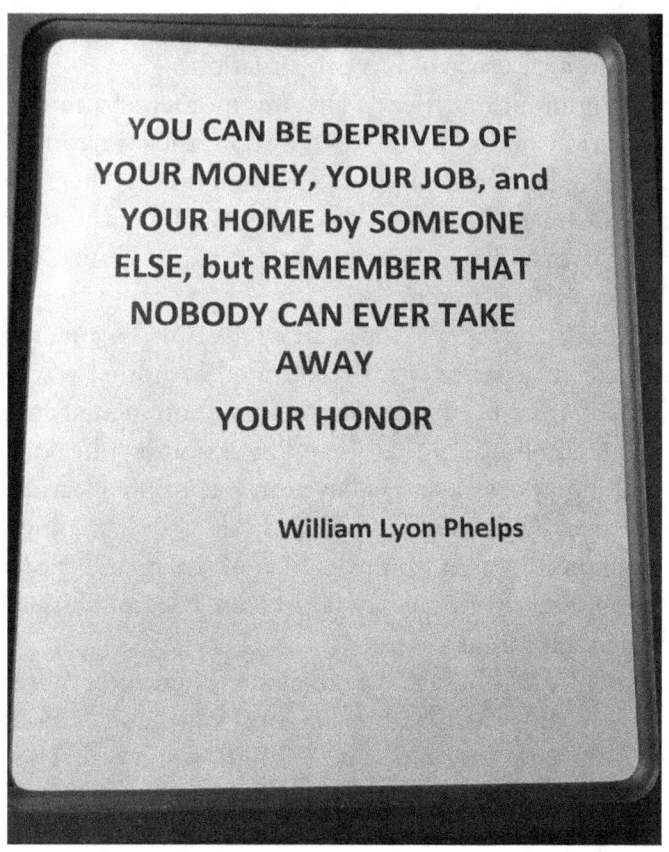

Back to the English Channel where our pilot is floating in the water, struggling to stay alive. His knife has now become his most prized possession, as he needs it to cut away the chords of the parachute that delivered him to this water. He cuts a small section of it, temporarily laying it over his shoulder. Next, he pulls the fabric of the chute close, cutting a section of it.

Knowing his short endurance of being able to tread water, he manages to trap some air with the material. He then uses the chord to tie the edges together, forming a makeshift life preserver. Very crude, but he feels confident it will keep him afloat for a while.

Floating in relatively mild swells, he listens for any sign of watercraft. "Lord if it be your will to take me today, please make it be painless", he prays.

Now, the British people were well-informed of the threat of the Nazi war machine. If I may put in a plug for the movie, "Miracle at Dunkirk", it portrayed the desperate situation of the French, Belgian, British, and Dutch soldiers as they were driven back to the beaches of Dunkirk by the relentless Nazis. Watch the movie to see the ending, but it points out the realization that the whole country had to work together in the war effort.

Our pilot, exhausted by this time, is unaware of the numerous civilians that he cannot see on the shore. They saw the fighter plane hit the water and had sent several small boats out to see if a pilot was onboard. The plane might be salvaged later – they were now searching the waters for the pilot.

Fighting to stay conscious, the desperate pilot hears voices in the distance. He barks out the loudest yell he can manage, raising his arm at the same time, in a wave. "Over there!" ...it's the sweetest phrase he ever heard, and then a small boat approaches. His countrymen pull him out of the water and into the fishing boat. "God forgive me if my faith ever faltered" were the words he stated, as he remembered the phrase, "for we walk by faith, not by sight".

YOUR JOURNEY

I used to have a picture of an owl over my desk with the phrase along the bottom, "I may not know all the answers, but I know someone that does." Being in the teaching profession for approximately 40 years, I can appreciate the truthfulness of that phrase. My tendency is to keep my distance from anyone who claims to know everything; the self-proclaimed "experts". On the other hand, I do strive to learn from the mistakes of others or from the experience of others.

Learning is a natural process and each one of us learns at our own pace. With the advent of the smartphone, we have access to all kinds of information on endless subjects. There are some who believe that Google has all the answers. I won't argue against information being available at your fingertips, but I see a dangerous trend with this.

My concern has been heightened by a recent report about mental health in the United States. According to the Journal of Abnormal Psychology, there was a 63% increase in young adults between the ages of 18 and 25 reporting symptoms of depression between 2009 and 2017. The study also showed significant increases in the rates of young adults who reported serious psychological distress and suicidal thoughts or suicide-related outcomes during similar time periods. This is very alarming!

Walk into any airport terminal or other public place and it becomes obvious how dependent people are on their electronic devices. Communicating with family and friends is a good thing. On the other hand, constantly staring at your cellphone sends a message that you have no social skills; that your device is more important than those around you.

We are social beings. That is the way The Good Lord created us. The cell phone, obviously, is a great convenience. It is not there for the purpose of filling your brain with all kinds of random information so that you can sound smart when you converse with... Wait! Do you converse with anybody or are you always staring at that device?

For many, therein lies the problem. I am no psychologist, but I think it is safe to say that your demeanor, your personality, has much to do with what you put into or what you allow into your brain.

It is amazing and even overwhelming how much email shows up on a daily basis, not to mention the distraction of random "pop-ups". While we are nearly forced to be available via email in this highly-technical world, we need to shut off much of that by "unsubscribing". It's a busy, crazy world with new technology potentially attacking our sanity on a daily basis.

Are you near that deep pit? Are you holding your own, but treading the edge, just hoping you can avoid the fall?

Been there ...I have been there, inside that pit, which is my motivation for sharing my story. The Pit, or the Rut, if you prefer that term, is a horrible place to be. Nobody chooses to be there. Most, as was my experience, find themselves there, unprepared as to how to climb out.

Let's go back to our World War II pilot who felt so alone floating in the water of The English Channel. He recognized that he was in peril. He knew that it was doubtful he would be able to survive on his own.

Two actions he took that were so critical were that blind call of "Mayday" over the radio, then that shout from the water to let others know he was in peril. God knew there were people (...perhaps angels) in place who would do everything possible to rescue him. He knew he had to hang onto that faith that The Lord had better plans for him. (if one has faith the size of a mustard seed...).

If substance abuse caused your rut, then make a determination to overcome it. Write it down and place a date on it. Consider going to the website for substance abuse treatment locator. Lean on your friends as much as you can, first making sure they are your true friend.

YOU CANNOT OVERCOME IT ALONE

◆

Maybe you are feeling pressure of choosing a career. There are career counselors who can assist with that, steer you in the right direction, based on your interests. Don't assume you can do everything from your computer or smartphone. Use those to find your way to the counselor, the human being that can help you.

Perhaps college is not for you. There is plenty of demand for technical jobs that need to be filled. Talk to friends or relatives about your interests, then look into the possibilities.

Maybe the loss of a loved one is keeping you in a state of depression. That's a tough situation that will require time. You need friends, true friends who can give you encouragement. Be very particular about what you choose to listen to, be it the radio, CD, iPod, etc. There are many artists out there who produce encouraging music, the input our brains need in order to confront the obstacles of a challenging world.

Have you accepted a position in a new location where nothing is familiar? Perhaps you left your friends behind and you feel lonely, maybe even unsure of your decision to relocate. My grandmother used to give me advice similar to "You need to find a church and get involved, make new friends…" It seems I had to try to do it all on my own when I was young, before I realized how much wisdom was given to me in those words. There is much evil in this world and none of us is spared the struggle of trying to find our place; to fulfill our destiny.

Social media is available to us, but it just cannot compare to being in a room with other humans that have beliefs similar to ours. We were meant to be encouraging to each other, to share a smile that might help our neighbor get through his or her day. As I stated earlier when referring to my owl picture, " I don't know all the answers..." You know what? There is no fellow earthling on this planet of ours that does know all the answers, that can even predict with certainty whether or not tomorrow will arrive.

Keep in mind that the Pit is there, ready to take any one of us who may unwillingly find ourselves falling into it. As God's children, we must always be diligent and be respectful of others who, though not showing it on the outside, could be traversing the edge of that Pit. We must be ready to extend a hand to those we discover who need to climb back out.

"Be watchful, stand firm in your faith, be courageous, be strong."

ABOUT THE AUTHOR

◆

Kelly Martin gained new insight into the pursuit of purpose through recognizing the irreplaceable encouragement and companionship of friends and relatives. Climbing out of his own "pit" following a divorce, he worked at regaining his positive attitude, which kept him moving during adversities. Not always strong in his faith that God had his back, he continues to move forward, praying each day for God's help and direction.

Having survived through the struggles and several temporary jobs he describes in his book, he learned to appreciate the challenges of people in many roles, whether it be the person checking out groceries, serving ice cream, driving a truck…any one of a variety of occupations. He has learned to be a much better listener, as it seems there are not enough of us willing to spend time listening to our fellow members of The Journey we call life.

After obtaining his Bachelor of Science degree in Aviation, he obtained experience in over thirty different models of aircraft. His passengers have included coaches, Special Olympics team members, governors, and government officials. Having flown regularly in business jets at high altitudes, he feels closest to God while on the ground, surrounded by fellow believers. His past experience enables him to take the role of encourager to friends or relatives going through their struggles.

In order to be recognized in this world of ours, it seems one has to be exceptionally talented or beautiful. There is not enough recognition given to those who go about their daily lives, being dedicated to their job and to their family, living responsibly and honorably. None of us is perfect, but through perseverance, we can each strive for that goal.

Remembering one Christmas spent with only his Min-Pin, Max, Kelly now lives with his wife, Judy, in Danville, Indiana. He is very aware of and thankful for God's blessings, several of those in the form of grandchildren. Many of those blessings seemed impossible but are rewards for hanging onto that little seed of Faith.

Life after recovering and then meeting Judy can be summed up in the expression on the face of Hank, a great kid and one we met through the foster care system.

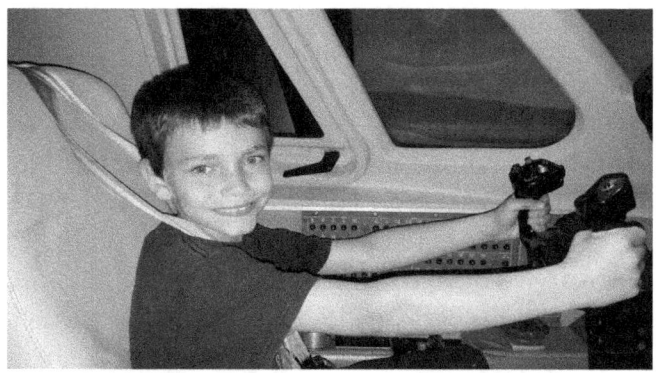

www.ingramcontent.com/pod-product-compliance
Lightning Source LLC
LaVergne TN
LVHW011738060526
838200LV00051B/3222